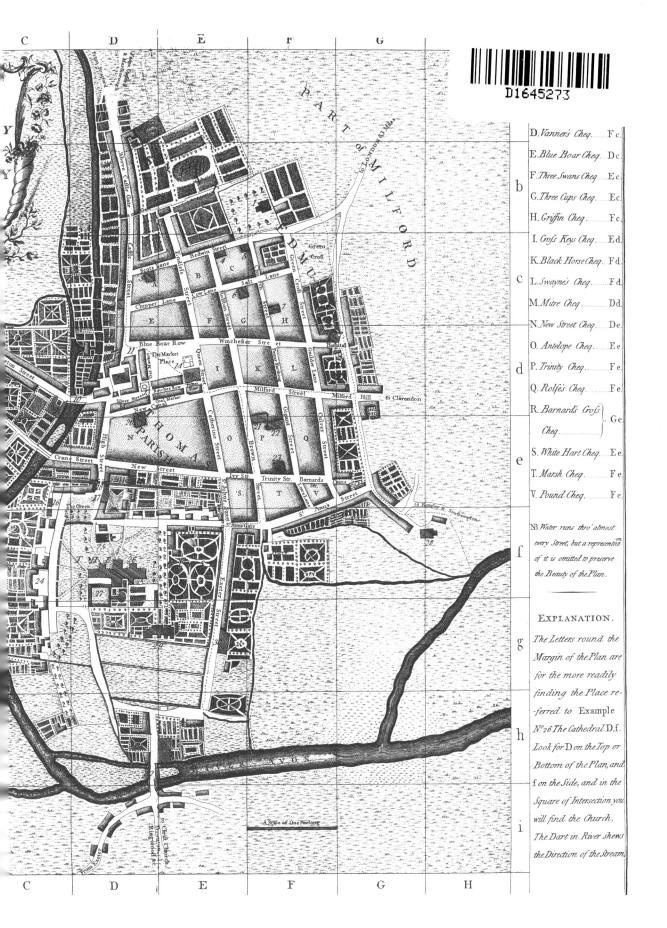

D1645273

D. *Vanner's Cheq.* ... F c.
E. *Blue Boar Cheq.* ... D c.
F. *Three Swans Cheq.* ... E c.
G. *Three Cups Cheq.* ... E c.
H. *Griffin Cheq.* ... F c.
I. *Cross Keys Cheq.* ... E d.
K. *Black Horse Cheq.* ... F d.
L. *Swayne's Cheq.* ... F d.
M. *Mitre Cheq.* ... D d.
N. *New Street Cheq.* ... D e.
O. *Antelope Cheq.* ... E e.
P. *Trinity Cheq.* ... E e.
Q. *Rolfe's Cheq.* ... F e.
R. *Barnard's Cross Cheq.* } ... G e.
S. *White Hart Cheq.* ... E e.
T. *Marsh Cheq.* ... F e.
V. *Pound Cheq.* ... F e.

N.B. *Water runs thro' almost every Street, but a representation of it is omitted to preserve the Beauty of the Plan.*

EXPLANATION.

The Letters round the Margin of the Plan are for the more readily finding the Place referred to Example Nº 26 The Cathedral D.f. Look for D on the Top or Bottom of the Plan, and f on the Side, and in the Square of Intersection you will find the Church. The Dart in River shews the Direction of the Stream.

A Scale of One Furlong

SALISBURY
PAST

Watercolour of the Poultry Cross and market, pre-1852; artist unknown.

SALISBURY
PAST

Ruth Newman & Jane Howells

Ruth Newman

Jane Howells

Phillimore

2001

Published by
PHILLIMORE & CO. LTD.
Shopwyke Manor Barn, Chichester, West Sussex

ISBN 1 86077 177 7

Printed and bound in Great Britain by
BIDDLES LTD.
Guildford, Surrey

Contents

List of illustrations   vii

Acknowledgements   ix

I   The Need to Move
page 1

II   Building a New City
page 7

III   Growth and Prosperity
page 21

IV   New Ideas and Challenges
page 33

V   Coping with Change
page 41

VI   An Elegant Society
page 57

VII   Progress in Difficult Times
page 73

VII   Adapting to a Modern World
page 95

VIII   An Eventful Century
page 111

Select Bibliography   129

Index   131

List of Illustrations

Frontispiece: The Poultry Cross

1. View of Old Sarum and the city _____ 1
2. Map showing the location of Old Sarum _____ 2
3. View from the ramparts of Old Sarum _____ 2
4. Coin of Ethelred, minted at Old Sarum _____ 3
5. Bishop Roger's tomb, Salisbury Cathedral _____ 3
6. Plan of burgage plots _____ 4
7. St Martin's church _____ 5
8. Aerial photograph of Old Sarum _____ 6
9. Leaden Hall _____ 7
10. View of Salisbury Cathedral from the south _____ 8
11. The North Canonry _____ 8
12. Naish's map of Salisbury _____ 9
13. Mitre House _____ 10
14. Castle Street Gate plaque _____ 10
15. Water channels in Minster Street _____ 11
16. City ramparts _____ 12
17. Ayleswade/Harnham Bridge _____ 12
18. Chapel of St John _____ 13
19. St Thomas's church _____ 13
20. A preaching friar _____ 14
21. Hospital of St Nicholas _____ 14
22. Brethren of the Hospital of St Nicholas _____ 15
23. Trinity Hospital _____ 16
24. Papal Bull, Trinity Hospital _____ 16
25. William Russel's House _____ 17
26. Salisbury Market Place _____ 18
27. Street names _____ 19
28. The Poultry Cross _____ 19
29. Sheep in the Market _____ 20
30. Crane Street _____ 21
31. Old Wiltshire horned sheep _____ 22
32. Cloth making processes _____ 22
33. Harnham Mill _____ 22
34. The hall of John Halle _____ 23
35. Interior of John Halle's hall _____ 24
36. Ward list, 1399-1400 _____ 24
37. A saddler _____ 25
38. Pilgrim's badge, Thomas Becket _____ 26
39. House opposite the Poultry Cross _____ 27
40. The Joiners' Guildhall _____ 27
41. The Shoemakers' Guildhall _____ 27
42. Merchants' marks _____ 28
43. The Giant _____ 29
44. High Street Gate _____ 31
45. The Close wall in Exeter Street _____ 31
46. No. 49 New Canal _____ 32
47. John Halle _____ 32
48. Hemingsby _____ 33
49. Fisherton Anger church _____ 34
50. Plaque to three martyrs _____ 34
51. Aula le Stage _____ 35
52. De Vaux College _____ 35
53. Doom painting in St Thomas's church _____ 36
54. St Thomas's church without Doom painting ____ 37
55. Choristers' Schoolroom _____ 38
56. The Greencroft _____ 39
57. John Speed map _____ 40
58. Portrait of Joan Popley _____ 41
59. A beggar _____ 52
60. Water channels in Castle Street _____ 43
61. John Ivie's 'Declaration' _____ 44
62. Plaque to John Ivie _____ 44
63. Survey of poor, 1635 _____ 45
64. Church House _____ 46
65. Portrait of Edward Ludlow _____ 47
66. Longford Castle _____ 48
67. The Bell Tower _____ 48
68. Pillaging soldier _____ 49
69. St Edmund's church _____ 51
70. The Bishop's Palace _____ 51
71. Portrait of Colonel John Penruddock _____ 52
72. High Street Gate _____ 53
73. Christopher Wren's notebook _____ 53
74. The *George Inn* _____ 53
75. An inventory of 1685 _____ 54
76. The College of Matrons _____ 55

77. Blechynden's Almhouses _____ 55
78. Taylor's Almshouses _____ 55
79. Places of care and control _____ 56
80. A trade token _____ 57
81. Printing a local newspaper _____ 57
82. A balloon _____ 58
83. Barnard's Cross House _____ 58
84. Portrait of James Harris _____ 59
85. Malmesbury House _____ 59
86. Benjamin Banks' instruments _____ 60
87. The Assembly Rooms _____ 61
88. The College _____ 62
89. The Hall, New Street _____ 62
90. No. 44 St Ann's Street _____ 63
91. Nos. 36-38 St Ann's Street _____ 63
92. No. 18 St Ann's Street _____ 63
93. The Infirmary_____ 65
94. Plan of Salisbury–Southampton Canal _____ 66
95. Fisherton Toll House _____ 67
96. Inn yard at Salisbury _____ 67
97. The Winterslow Hut _____ 68
98. Elizabethan Council House fire _____ 69
99. Demolition of the Bishop's Guildhall _____ 70
100. The Guildhall _____ 70
101. James Wyatt _____ 71
102. The Bell Tower _____ 72
103. Railway cottages _____ 73
104. Trade card – umbrellas _____ 74
105. Trade card – cutlery _____ 74
106. Salisbury's Exhibition, 1852 _____ 75
107. Malthouses _____ 75
108. Joseph Lovibond_____ 76
109. Crane Street Workhouse _____ 76
110. Settlement examination _____ 77
111. Salisbury Union Workhouse _____ 78
112. Radnor House _____ 79
113. The Clock Tower and Infirmary _____ 79
114. An anti-Papal demonstration _____ 80
115. Billhead – Tasker's Agricultural Machinery _____ 81
116. Special constables _____ 81
117. The Parliament Stone _____ 82
118. Reform cordial_____ 82
119. December 1832 election _____ 83
120. Detail of water channels in Minster Street _____ 84
121. Extract from 1851 report on cholera _____ 85
122. Toone's Court_____ 85
123. Salisbury Infirmary _____ 86
124. Laverstock House _____ 87
125. Laverstock House certificate of admission _____ 87
126. Salisbury Electric Light and Supply Company _____ 88
127. Plan of St Edmund's School _____ 89
128. Portrait of Henry Hatcher _____ 90

129. Training College students _____ 91
130. Railway accident, 1856 _____ 92
131. The London train at Fisherton station _____ 93
132. The Market House interior _____ 93
133. The Market House exterior _____ 94
134. Map showing boundary changes _____ 95
135. The Police _____ 96
136. Advertisement for Scout Motors _____ 97
137. General election, 1950 _____ 97
138. St Edmund's Church Street Methodist church _____ 99
139. 1881 poster _____ 100
140. Chipper Lane Library _____ 101
141. The Museum _____ 102
142. Archery _____ 102
143. Visitors at Old Sarum _____ 103
144. Henry and William Fawcett _____ 104
145. Victoria Park, 1902 _____ 104
146. Queen Victoria's Jubilee, 1887 _____ 105
147. Coronation dinner, 1902 _____ 106
148. Places of entertainment _____ 108
149. The Odeon _____ 109
150. The Playhouse _____ 109
151. Railway disaster, 1906_____ 110
152. Carriers' carts _____ 110
153. Recruiting Office _____ 111
154. Ladies' sewing party _____ 112
155. First World War advertisement _____ 113
156. Council houses _____ 113
157. Fulford Place _____ 114
158. The General Strike _____ 115
159. Scout van _____ 115
160. St Mark's roundabout _____ 116
161. Park and ride _____ 116
162. High Street shops _____ 117
163. New Sarum Operatic Society programme _____ 117
164. School in wartime _____ 118
165. Salisbury Museum in wartime _____ 118
166. Charity concert, 1943_____ 119
167. VE day _____ 120
168. Prefabs _____ 120
169. Salisbury Close, 1945 _____ 121
170. Futuristic plan for Salisbury _____ 122
171. Floods _____ 122
172. Tribbeck's shop, 1911 _____ 123
173. Watsons shop, 1953_____ 123
174. Sculpture on Choristers' Green _____ 124
175. Sundial in St Thomas's Square _____ 124
176. West Front, Salisbury Cathedral _____ 125
177. Mrs. Jesse's shop _____ 125
178. Housing in Gigant Street _____ 126
179. The Michaelmas Fair _____ 127
180. The Cathedral from Long Bridge _____ 128

Acknowledgements

Illustrations have been reproduced in this volume by kind permission of the following: The Ashmolean Museum, Oxford, 65; Avon Lodge Veterinary Practice, 95; The Bodleian Library, University of Oxford, 20; The British Library, 68; Michael Charlton, 77, 78; Peter Fawcett, 108, 144; Grand Western Archery Society and South Wilts Archery Club, 142; Hampshire Record Office, 84, 85; Jenny Hiley, 6, 42, 90, 91, 92; Joe Newman, 3, 9, 14, 16, 23, 24, 27, 34, 39, 45, 46, 50, 58, 71, 80, 83, 86, 88, 89, 103, 117, 156, 161, 174, 175, 176, 178; National Monuments Record, 8; The National Portrait Gallery, 101; National Trust, 71; David Robson ABIPP, 53, 160; St Thomas's Church, 53; Salisbury and South Wilts Museum, frontispiece, 1, 4, 15, 38, 43, 60, 96, 97, 99, 104, 105, 106, 114, 115, 120, 128, 130, 151, 153, 159, 163, 165, 166; from the Lovibond Collection (housed at the Museum, owned by Salisbury District Council), 17, 29, 157, 162, 179; Salisbury Cathedral Fabric Records, 73, 101; Salisbury City Almshouse and Welfare Charities, 24, 58, 77, 78; Salisbury District Council, 44, 58, 62, 170; *Salisbury Journal*, 136, 155, 158; Salisbury Medical Society, 123; the late Alan Bedenham of the Salvation Army, 139; Southampton Archive Services, 94; Bill Toop, 135, 150; Winifred Towner, 164; Tribbecks, 145, 172; Mary Underwood, 56, 87, 107, 111, 118, 137, 171, 177; Peter Walker, 80; Watsons, 25, 173; Wiltshire and Swindon Record Office, 22, 36, 37, 67, 75, 81, 98, 100, 109, 110, 112, 119, 121, 122, 125, 127, 129, 131, 138, 141, 146, 147, 167, 168, 169; Wiltshire County Council Heritage and Libraries, 126, 140, 143, 154, 180; Wiltshire Heritage Library, 61; Wiltshire Record Society, 63. Other illustrations have been taken from Benson and Hatcher, Dodsworth, Hall and Heape.

Every effort has been made to contact copyright holders, and we apologise if any have been missed.

Our families, friends and colleagues near and far have entered into this project with great enthusiasm. They provided support and encouragement whenever we flagged, and showed admirable patience when we became obsessed.

Time, information, advice and skills were generously given by the following, for which we are most grateful: Graham Annetts; Fred Barlow; John Cox and Timothy Price at St Thomas's; Peter Fawcett; Steve Fear; Michael Franklin and Anita Goddard, Salisbury District Council; Peter Gillam, Salisbury Medical Society; Gillian Nolan, Salisbury City Almshouse and Welfare Charities; Karen Rudd at Mompesson House;

Joan Schmeising and Gemma Russell; Roy Spring, Salisbury Cathedral Fabric Records; Sheila Steffans; Rachel and Roland Tribbeck; John Waddington at the Medieval Hall; and the staff at Phillimore.

Special thanks go to Mary Underwood for generously letting us use so many of her late husband, Austin Underwood's, evocative photographs of Salisbury; and to Jenny Hiley for taking time out of her gap year to produce some delightful drawings.

There were times when we both almost became fixtures at Salisbury Local Studies Library where the expertise of Bruce Purvis and his colleagues added greatly to the effectiveness of our visits, and they always seemed pleased to see us.

Train rides to Trowbridge to the Record Office provided opportunities for intense discussion, and when we arrived we could rely on Steve Hobbs to throw light on our queries and suggest ever more lines of enquiry, and produce the relevant documents.

The journey to Salisbury Museum is much shorter but equally worthwhile. Jane Standen shared her intimate acquaintance of the collections and Peter Saunders found time (and space) in the hectic life of a modern museum director to advise us further, and approve of our choices.

Joe Newman has shared our frustrations and enjoyment, and has stoically word processed, proofread and taken photographs over a period of 16 months, remaining a source of strength throughout.

Above all, we would like to thank John Chandler, for getting us into this in the first place, for so willingly placing his knowledge and resources at our disposal, and still being our friend at the end!

The Need to Move

WHEN WILLIAM COBBETT rode down the Avon Valley in the hot August of 1826, he described Old Sarum as three cheeses 'laid one upon the other; the bottom one a great deal broader than the next, and the top one like a Stilton cheese in proportion to a Gloucester one'. To Cobbett it was 'this accursed hill', but any history of Salisbury has to look to its origins. The role of Old Sarum and the need to move are pivotal to the birth of the new city.

Old Sarum was built as an Iron-Age hill-fort in the 6th century B.C., one of several Celtic forts in the area probably used as emergency strongholds. The Romans, arriving in about A.D. 43, rejected the opportunity to turn *Sorviodunum* into a major town. The cramped conditions on the hill and the uncertain elements made them prefer the shelter of the small settlement of Stratford-sub-Castle to the west. However, Old Sarum was clearly an important point in their road network, a Roman 'Spaghetti Junction'. Its history in Saxon times is patchy. The Anglo-Saxon Chronicle records that in A.D. 552 a West Saxon chief 'Cynric' 'fought against the Britons at a place called *Searoburgh* and put them to flight'. After this Old Sarum was almost certainly abandoned for the best part of three centuries.

In 1003, Wilton, one of the most significant towns of Saxon Wessex, was sacked by the Danes. Some of the inhabitants fled, taking refuge inside the ramparts of Old Sarum. There they stayed and an urban community developed. The Norman Conquest brought more significant changes. The relatively small number of invaders meant that they

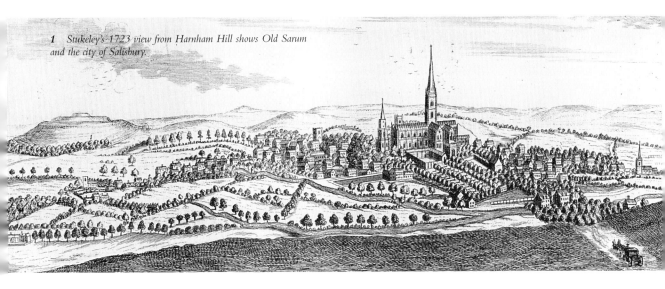

1 *Stukeley's 1723 view from Harnham Hill shows Old Sarum and the city of Salisbury.*

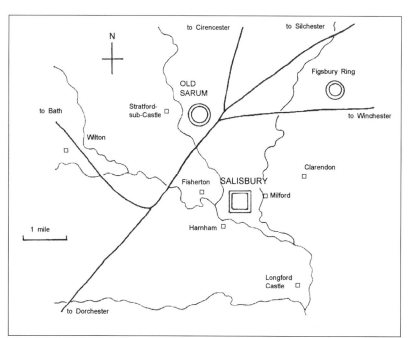

2   Old Sarum lies approximately 1½ miles north of the city of Salisbury and was built on a hill about 240 feet above and to the east of the spot where the River Avon was always fordable.

3   From the ramparts it is possible to see three of the Roman roads which met at Old Sarum. Particularly obvious is the road to the east through Ford to Winchester (Venta Belgarum).

had to build secure fortified sites to hold the country against Anglo-Saxon revolt. Old Sarum was already of strategic importance and the Normans realised its potential. It was used as an assembly point for William's armies and the hill-fort was transformed into a motte and bailey castle using forced labour from the local population. The original wooden keep on the motte was later rebuilt in stone and the remainder of the hill-fort interior became the bailey.

In 1086, the information from Domesday Book was probably presented to William at Old Sarum. A huge quantity of data on the people and lands of England had been collected to satisfy the king's need for knowledge of his conquered country. At the same time, on 1 August, Lammas Day, the principal noblemen gathered here to take an oath of loyalty to William enabling him to assert full authority over them.

In 1075 the decision had been taken to build a cathedral within the bailey ramparts. Bishop Herman

of Sherborne transferred his see to Old Sarum as a more central focus for a large diocese which extended from Berkshire to Dorset. It was at this time that the name *Sarisburia* or *Salisburia* came into common use and this was abbreviated by clerks to *Sarum*. The decision to share a site between the clergy and the military was to have far-reaching implications. Building began on the new cathedral under Bishop Herman to a typical Rhineland design with an apsidal end, and it was completed by his energetic successor the Norman Bishop (later Saint) Osmund. In 1092 the new cathedral was consecrated, but five days later it was struck by lightning and much of the east end was destroyed.

Early in the next century it was rebuilt and enlarged by another Norman, Bishop Roger, to a design based on the Abbaye aux Dames at Caen. A great builder, Roger planned Old Sarum castle as his residence and surrounded the cathedral and its close with a stone curtain wall so that the secular

4 Coin of Ethelred minted at Old Sarum. In the Saxon period a mint was established, striking coins bearing the name 'Serebrig'. Silver pennies were minted there until Henry II's reign (1154-89).

5 Bishop Roger's tomb, Salisbury Cathedral. Bishop Roger was first and foremost a powerful politician rather than a churchman, a man of great ambition who combined the roles of the military and religious in one person.

and the religious were confined within the Iron-Age ramparts. Roger's worldly ambitions led to his downfall during the civil war between Stephen and Matilda, after which the king appointed a military governor to be responsible for the castle, leaving the Bishop solely in control of the cathedral, with the distinct possibility of increasing conflict.

Old Sarum continued to grow outside the defences, where the Roman roads converged. It was once believed that the town lay within the ramparts but excavations in the 1950s and '60s have shown evidence of a large eastern suburb near the present *Old Castle Inn*. A medieval site was found with timber buildings, cess pits and a mass grave, plus a junction

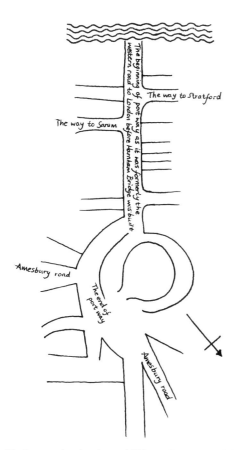

6 *The burgage plots, based on a 1680 map. Recent research has suggested that the plan of the rotten borough of Old Sarum reflects the boundaries of a southward extension to the town, which was laid out along the road to Stratford-sub-Castle.*

of roads and tracks. John Leland, the Tudor scholar and topographer stated, in 1540, that 'ther hath beene houses in tyme of mynd inhabited in the est suburbe of Old Saresbryi'. It is probable, therefore, that the town developed where the main roads met outside the East Gate, with further building to the west and south.

In the late 12th century the town appears to have been entering a period of decline. Few improvements were made to the cathedral, which was small in comparison with its neighbours, Winchester and Wells. A subsequent complaint, listed in the Papal Bull of 1218, stated that 'the fabric [of the cathedral] was so ruinous that it is a constant danger to the congregation which has dwindled to the extent that it is hardly able to provide for the repair of the roofs'. Wilton and other settlements in the valley attracted the inhabitants.

Although today Old Sarum and New Sarum are used to distinguish the deserted hilltop from the newly planned city, this was not always so. Domesday seems to show that there were already two areas bearing the name of *Sarisberie*: a manor or group of manors held by the bishop, and a borough paying dues to the king. Other documentary evidence supports the existence of two Salisburys in the 12th century, and indeed shows that the eventual move in 1220 was from the borough of Salisbury on the hill down to *old* Salisbury in the meadows by the river. Hamlets are thought to have existed around St Martin's church, and near a mill on the Avon just north of the new cathedral site, with possibly another where the river was habitually crossed at Harnham.

Momentous choices clearly had to be made. Should the clergy at Old Sarum improve and enlarge their cathedral or move to a more congenial site where there was space to expand and at the same time to establish a new town? Contemporary accounts endorse the view of Old Sarum's difficulties. One of the canons, Peter de Blois, is reputed to have said, 'What has the House of the Lord to do with

4 *Coin of Ethelred minted at Old Sarum. In the Saxon period a mint was established, striking coins bearing the name 'Serebrig'. Silver pennies were minted there until Henry II's reign (1154-89).*

5 *Bishop Roger's tomb, Salisbury Cathedral. Bishop Roger was first and foremost a powerful politician rather than a churchman, a man of great ambition who combined the roles of the military and religious in one person.*

and the religious were confined within the Iron-Age ramparts. Roger's worldly ambitions led to his downfall during the civil war between Stephen and Matilda, after which the king appointed a military governor to be responsible for the castle, leaving the Bishop solely in control of the cathedral, with the distinct possibility of increasing conflict.

Old Sarum continued to grow outside the defences, where the Roman roads converged. It was once believed that the town lay within the ramparts but excavations in the 1950s and '60s have shown evidence of a large eastern suburb near the present *Old Castle Inn*. A medieval site was found with timber buildings, cess pits and a mass grave, plus a junction

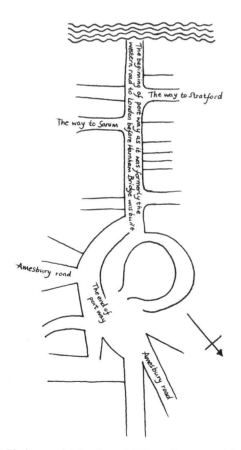

6 *The burgage plots, based on a 1680 map. Recent research has suggested that the plan of the rotten borough of Old Sarum reflects the boundaries of a southward extension to the town, which was laid out along the road to Stratford-sub-Castle.*

of roads and tracks. John Leland, the Tudor scholar and topographer stated, in 1540, that 'ther hath beene houses in tyme of mynd inhabited in the est suburbe of Old Saresbryi'. It is probable, therefore, that the town developed where the main roads met outside the East Gate, with further building to the west and south.

In the late 12th century the town appears to have been entering a period of decline. Few improvements were made to the cathedral, which was small in comparison with its neighbours, Winchester and Wells. A subsequent complaint, listed in the Papal Bull of 1218, stated that 'the fabric [of the cathedral] was so ruinous that it is a constant danger to the congregation which has dwindled to the extent that it is hardly able to provide for the repair of the roofs'. Wilton and other settlements in the valley attracted the inhabitants.

Although today Old Sarum and New Sarum are used to distinguish the deserted hilltop from the newly planned city, this was not always so. Domesday seems to show that there were already two areas bearing the name of *Sarisberie*: a manor or group of manors held by the bishop, and a borough paying dues to the king. Other documentary evidence supports the existence of two Salisburys in the 12th century, and indeed shows that the eventual move in 1220 was from the borough of Salisbury on the hill down to *old* Salisbury in the meadows by the river. Hamlets are thought to have existed around St Martin's church, and near a mill on the Avon just north of the new cathedral site, with possibly another where the river was habitually crossed at Harnham.

Momentous choices clearly had to be made. Should the clergy at Old Sarum improve and enlarge their cathedral or move to a more congenial site where there was space to expand and at the same time to establish a new town? Contemporary accounts endorse the view of Old Sarum's difficulties. One of the canons, Peter de Blois, is reputed to have said, 'What has the House of the Lord to do with

7   An early 19th-century view of St Martin's church. Some of the foundations have been dated at c.1100. When Bishop Osmund wrote of 'the Church of Sarum' in 1091, he was almost certainly referring to St Martin's. By the 12th century a settlement existed in the Milford area around the church. The angle of St Martin's Church Street suggests that it predates Salisbury's grid system of streets.

castles? Let us in God's name descend into the Plain.' William de Wanda, Dean of Sarum in 1220, described how Bishop Herbert Poore took the decision to move *before* 1200, but progress was slow because of financial problems and the death of the bishop in 1217. The idea was revived by his more famous brother, Bishop Richard Poore, and it was Richard who received the Papal blessing to remove the cathedral to a new site.

It is always difficult to distinguish fact from legend. An early 13th-century poem by Henry d'Avranches paints a picture of terminal misery and decline at Old Sarum and compares this with the beauties and wonders of New Sarum. At Old Sarum, 'nothing beautiful nor useful could grow there, nothing except wormwood … Little water was to be found, but chalk in abundance. The winds howled and no nightingales ever sang'. The chalk 'dazzled their eyes' and the lack of water 'provoked thirst'. Despite the florid style, this eye-witness account does seem to provide us with some authentic evidence. The writer would almost certainly have visited both the unfinished new cathedral and the partially demolished old one.

Incompatible neighbours and, more importantly, an inhospitable and inconvenient site in a confined area made expansion difficult. The clergy were determined to exaggerate the horrors of Old Sarum for the Pope in Rome and the extent of the hyperbole suggests determination, if not desperation, to move. A papal legate, Gualo, was instructed to investigate the complaints submitted to the Pope and he concluded that these were 'sufficiently proved'. The Papal Bull of 1218 summarised the grievances, omitting some of the more extreme ones. Nevertheless, the scarcity of water, and the harassment and interference by the guards were accepted and permission was granted for the move. Once the Papal blessing had been received, arrangements were made to proceed both with the building of the new cathedral in the valley below and with the organisation of a fund-raising campaign. Within 100 years, Old Sarum was a doomed city and little more than a quarry for building stone, although it continued to be represented in Parliament as a borough by two M.P.s – hence Cobbett's 'accursed hill'.

The siting of the new cathedral is also the subject of much folklore. Every Salisbury schoolchild 'knows'

8   *This aerial photograph of Old Sarum from the north shows the cathedral and the castle. Henry d'Avranches described the nub of the problem: 'The city stood in the castle and the castle in the city … This stood in that and that in this … Therefore they were not really two separate things … but as they were neither two nor one, they were one divided in two'!   © Crown Copyright. NMR*

that an archer fired an arrow from the ramparts of Old Sarum and where it landed, 1½ miles away to the south at Myrifield (Maryfield), the cathedral was built. In fact this legend dates only from the early 18th century. The most obvious site for the new cathedral was Wilton with its wealthy abbey. Another legend, from the 15th century, suggested that Bishop Poore's real desire was to marry the Abbess of Wilton, despite the conventions of the Catholic Church. This was developed as anti-Catholic propaganda in the 19th century, whereby the clerics from Old Sarum were said to visit the nuns at Wilton, remaining 'until late', and so, to avoid scandal, the bishop had moved elsewhere.

The truth, however, was much more simple: Bishop Poore owned Myrifield with its rich pastures and abundant water supply and therefore any profits which might accrue from a successful new town would come to the church. Bishop Poore was in fact extremely fortunate. The foundations of the cathedral are just four feet deep and would pass no modern building regulations. However, the structure rests on a natural gravel layer, 27 feet thick, which protects it from underground movement. Had it been built on the present Friary or Churchfields sites, the cathedral would have collapsed, but Bishop Poore's inspired vision meant that the history of modern Salisbury was about to begin.

II

Building a New City

IT WAS NOT VIRGIN SOIL that received the beginnings of a new cathedral in 1220, but 'a fair mead of exceeding beauty' which met the requirements which had been so lacking at Old Sarum. To provide a focus for the religious life of the new community, a small wooden chapel was built during the summer of 1219, and consecrated on Trinity Sunday. On 28 April 1220, five foundation stones were laid 'in the presence of a great multitude of the common folk'. The vast scale of Richard Poore's new plans placed great demands on resources, both material and human. Numerous craftsmen working in stone, wood, metal and glass contributed their skills. Most remain nameless, though Nicholas of Ely was master mason working under the architect and clerk of works, Canon Elias de Dereham. Funds were raised across the country and benefactors gave materials: Alice Brewer of Dorset donated Purbeck marble for 12 years and the king supplied timber from the nearby royal forest of Clarendon.

Within five years the first part of the new cathedral was completed. On an occasion of great symbolic significance, the bodies of three earlier bishops, including Osmund, were brought down from the old cathedral for reinterment. The cathedral itself was consecrated in 1258 in the presence of King Henry III. It is not possible to date precisely the subsequent stages of construction, but it is likely that work continued as the infrastructure and craftsmen were already assembled. The cloisters and chapter house, and the separate bell tower followed

the main building, together with the addition of the spire for which Salisbury Cathedral is so renowned.

Richard Poore appreciated the importance for the cathedral of the community within which it grew. In the immediate vicinity of the increasingly magnificent building, he organised the allocation of plots with generous gardens to the key office holders of the church and urged them to demonstrate their support for the venture by building appropriate residences. Canons and vicars had to build at their own expense, and it is clear that by 1222 not all had even begun when the chapter decreed that 'everyone who has a site must begin to build to some purpose by Whitsuntide next ensuing or failing this the bishop shall dispose of his site'.

9 *Leaden Hall was known as 'Aula Plumbea' because of its lead roof. The original canon's residence on this site was built by Elias de Dereham, the cathedral architect, and completed in 1232. A frequent visitor in the early 19th century was John Constable and several of his works were painted while staying at the house.*

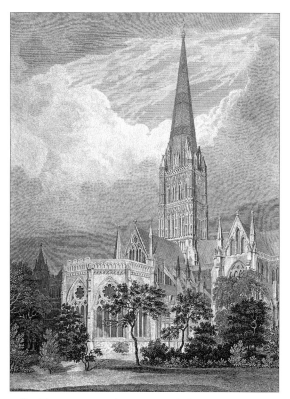

10 The spire presented an immense challenge to the builders, especially as the additional weight had not been considered when the original structure was designed. External flying buttresses and internal pillars and arches took the strain.

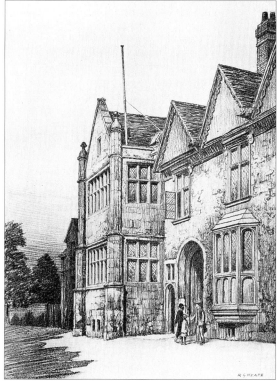

11 The North Canonry. The canons were urged to demonstrate their support for the new cathedral by building appropriate residences. Some evidence of the splendour of these original houses can still be seen.

Beyond the ditch which marked the boundary of the Close until the present stone wall was built between 1227 and 1242 the street plan for a new city was laid out. The design was determined by the cathedral itself, the river, and the main routes entering the area from the four points of the compass. Within that framework the streets and chequers were arranged in a roughly rectangular pattern which can still be clearly identified today.

The precise order of establishing the street layout is uncertain, but it is thought likely that the lane linking the existing community around St Martin's church to the cathedral formed the basis from which other early streets led. The grid pattern was considered the most efficient way of dividing the land to maximise street frontage. The standard size of a tenement was 7 by 3 perches (38.5 by 16.5 yards), and the bishop's tenants renting these plots paid 6d. at Easter and at Michaelmas. It is likely that many of the tenements were rapidly subdivided and occupied by several families. Recent archaeological evidence suggests a more complex development than was once thought, with archways giving access to buildings behind those constructed with street frontages on the perimeters of the chequers. Watercourses running along the streets were to be a key advantage of the new city over its predecessor. The necessity for the water to flow from the river along the level ground influenced the planning of the street layout.

The relationship between the bishop and the citizens of Salisbury was first set out in March 1225,

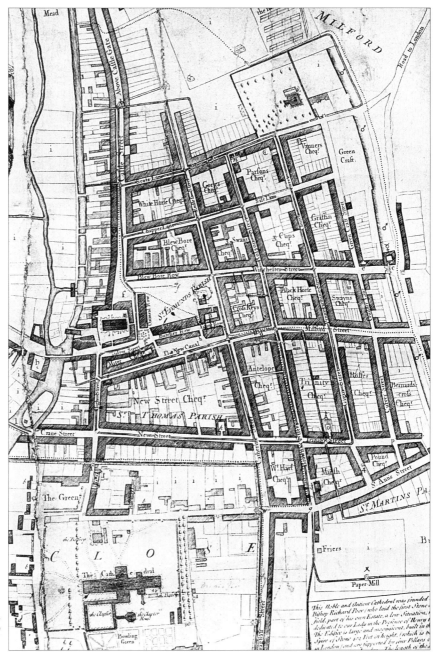

12 *The chequers are clearly shown in the Naish map, revised edition of 1751.*

when the size of the tenements in the city, together with the rents payable and the rights and obligations due were specified. The tenants were free to give, sell or mortgage their land, but it was prohibited to bequeath land to bodies such as religious commu-

nities to prevent wealth passing out of the bishop's control. In 1227 Henry III, who had shown a personal interest in the establishment of the new town from the beginning, granted two new charters. These confirmed the bishop's position as lord of the

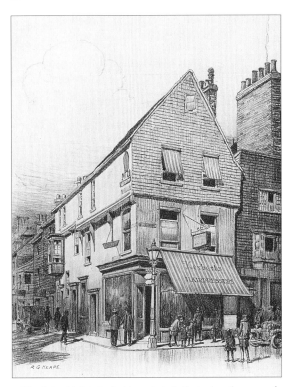

13 *It is said that the first house to be built stood on the corner of New Street – another contender for the first 'new street' of the city – and the modern High Street. This tradition is maintained by each successive bishop robing here in Mitre House before his enthronement.*

14 *Much of the Castle Street Gate was demolished in 1788. Its site is marked by this plaque.*

manor and secured for the citizens freedom from tolls and other duties throughout the king's demesnes, together with 'all liberties and quittances of the men of Winchester', a comparison which suggests optimism for the future of Salisbury.

Building the city defences was a tale of procrastination and indecision. The Charter of 1227 laid down the need for barriers on the north and east sides of Salisbury, the south and west being bound by the river. Bars were placed across the main roads at the outer end of both Milford Street and St Ann's Street, and stone gates were erected at the eastern end of the present Winchester Street (the Wyneman Gate) and at the northern boundary of Castle Street, where the water channel entered. Leland, travelling through Salisbury in 1542, 'recalled seeing one or two stone gates in the town' and both are shown on Naish's map of 1716. The three main bridges would have had bars across them where tolls were charged on merchandise entering the city. Despite the powers given to enclose the city, little defensive work was carried out for 200 years and then only intermittently. The walls were never built. A rampart and ditch were begun in the marshy area of Bugmore in the late 14th century but vandals came at night and broke part of the work. Further concern was expressed at the time of Agincourt in 1415, when property owners were asked to pay for the ditches then under construction, but not until 1440 was the money finally raised to complete the work. The corporation minutes record contributions in summer 1441: 'to finish the ditch around the city, William Swayne £1, John Wyot 6s 8d …'; and after the calculations 'there remained 12s 8d for the said ditch which William Warwyk the mayor paid … to the labourers working on the ditch'. From the late 15th century

15 *Early 19th-century view of the water channels in Minster Street. A 17th-century visitor saw 'pleasant little rivoletts which are knee deepe gliding sweetly through her bowels, to wash and clense them' though Defoe a century later found the streets 'full of wet and filth and weeds'.*

16   Today, the only reminders of the city ramparts are the name Rampart Road and this substantial mound in the Council House grounds.

the need to maintain the defences declined, and excavations in Milford Street showed that the ditch was filled in during the 15th and 16th centuries. Naish's map shows city ramparts along only the eastern side of the city and by the 19th century few fragments survived.

Just as the main roads of southern England were of significance to Old Sarum, the prosperity of the new city was also to depend on trade and it needed to be on the important routes. To encourage traffic, the river crossings had to be bridges rather than fords. The construction of a new bridge at Harnham just to the south of the cathedral both smoothed access to the city from that direction and attracted westerly traffic away from Wilton and into Salisbury. Ayles-wade Bridge was built by Bishop Bingham in 1244 and contributed significantly to Salisbury's prosperity. Bridges linking the city with its older neighbour Fisherton to the west were also constructed: the Lower Bridge in Crane Street in about 1300 and the Upper Bridge in Fisherton Street in 1318.

Former residents from Old Sarum, together with the workforce at the cathedral and their dependents, soon formed the nucleus of an urban population.

Increased numbers of people are suggested by the division of the city into three parishes in 1269. St Martin's parish, whose church pre-dates the cathedral, was initially outside the city boundary. The church of St Thomas dates from the time of the beginning of the cathedral and is first mentioned in 1238. There was also a need for a new third parish to the north by the 1260s. The building of the church of St Edmund of Abingdon (formerly Edmund Rich, treasurer of the cathedral 1222-34) had begun in about 1264. Founded by Bishop de la Wyle, this was a collegiate church, intended from the start to serve both the parish and the provost and 13 priests of the college. When the parish boundaries were formally established in 1269, the northern limit of St Edmund's lay outside the original line of the city

17 *Ayleswade Bridge was described by Leland in 1542 as 'a large and substantial structure with six great stone arches. Here, at the western end of this bridge, and divided from it by only the distance of a small island, is another bridge of four attractive arches'.*

18 *At the same time a chapel to St John the Baptist was built on this island, and the upkeep of both chapel and bridge were made the responsibility of the nearby Hospital of St Nicholas.*

ramparts, incorporating a 13th-century suburb. These three parish churches provided a focus for daily and weekly religious observance and, together with other institutions, gave religious succour to the citizens, both in life and death.

In the late 1220s a group of Franciscan, or Grey, Friars arrived in Salisbury. Bishop Poore supported the foundation of a house on a site to the east of the Close, and King Henry III was a generous benefactor of building materials. Lay bequests followed and the community expanded, with chapel, cloister, chapter house, infirmary and gardens. It achieved sufficient status for the English Provincial Chapter to meet there in 1393 and 1510, the former occasion honoured by the presence of Richard II who 'splendidly feasted' in stark contrast to the usual

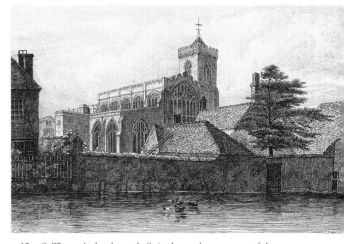

19 *St Thomas's church was built in the south-west corner of the area originally allocated for the market, and near to the presumed settlement at the mill of the original Salisbury. Its location was also important in the early years of the new city as it was clearly visible on the approach from the west along the road from Wilton.*

20   A Preaching Friar. The reputation of the friars for caring concern was reinforced by such descriptions as 'In the custodia of Salisbury over which Brother Stephen was president, the affection of mutual love flourished especially, for he himself was of so sweet a nature and of such joyousness ... that he never allowed anyone so far as it was in his power, to be sad.'

austere lifestyle of the friars whose role in the town was to help the poor and sick. The Grey Friars were also teachers and preachers and in this regard they were joined by the Dominican, or Black, Friars. A new house of Dominicans had been established with wealthy patrons at Wilton in 1245, but this proved to be a poor choice of location. Wilton was already suffering competition from the growth of Salisbury and within 40 years the convent moved three miles to the east just outside the city boundary across Fisherton Bridge.

The two friaries were often remembered in the wills of local people in acknowledgement of their power to intervene on behalf of souls. In 1406, Alice, widow of William Teynterer and wife of George Merriot, left to each house a bowl for drinking. Not all their interventions were spiritual, however: in 1318 a condemned man was being taken through Fisherton on his way to the gallows, and five of the friars, believing the verdict to be unjust, rescued the prisoner by force, allowing him to escape from the officers of the court. They were subsequently pardoned by the king. Nothing remains today of the house of the Dominican Friars; the neighbourhood known as the Friary marks the Franciscans' establishment, and it is thought some of the stonework is incorporated in walls of later buildings in the area.

The origins of the Hospital of St Nicholas are unclear, but its foundation is associated with Bishop Poore. Bishop Bingham made extensive alterations to its constitution and buildings in the 1230s, at around the same time as he constructed Ayleswade Bridge and St John's chapel. These three institutions were brought under common patronage, with a warden and other officers responsible for their administration and upkeep. The income from endowments of property in the city and elsewhere supported the employees and cared for the poor and the sick. The unusual layout of the church, with a double aisle divided by a central seven-arched arcade, may have been designed to provide for male and female inmates, or to separate inmates from parishioners. Further changes altered the functions

21   The Hospital of St Nicholas continues to function as an almshouse today; the modern range of buildings includes part of the original church and remnants of the early 13th-century predecessor to Bishop Bingham's foundation.

of St Nicholas closer to those of an almshouse providing pensions and accommodation for the elderly and destitute. Like other similar institutions it suffered from time to time from lack of income due to falling rents and maladministration. Statutes of 1478 provided 7s. 6d. a week between 12 men and women, plus 16 wagon loads of wood and one of coal yearly. Amongst the responsibilities of the master was the saying or singing of daily services, the provision of a barber and a laundress, and punishment of the faults of the residents – the most usual were quarrelling and living together in one room when unmarried!

The Hospital of the Holy Trinity was probably founded about 1370. Legend has it that Agnes Bottenham, keeper of an inn and a brothel, established the hospital as a penance to redeem her soul and her name does appear in early documents. She died in 1379 and one of her executors, John Chandler, set out additional rules for the hospital in 1394 to the extent that he too is described as its founder. Twelve poor people could be accommodated permanently and an additional 18 could stay up to three days, or longer if they were ill. The income came from rents from the hospital's property in the city, supplemented by offerings in the chapel, and the proceeds of the inmates' right to beg in the streets. An inventory of 1418 lists 28 beds, 25 coverlets, 13 quilts and 23 pairs of sheets. A varied diet was supplied: mutton, pork or beef on Sundays, Mondays, Tuesdays and Thursdays, fresh or salted fish on other days. The salaries of the sub-warden and the chaplain were fixed in the 15th century and were still at the same level in the 18th century. The inmates were required

22   Brethren and Sisters at the Hospital of St Nicholas. Detailed regulations were laid down, from the requirement that the four priests wear uniform russet cloaks, to the celebration of masses for the souls of benefactors and residents.

23 The history of Trinity Hospital suggests sound, efficient organisation and consistent provision of shelter and food for the needy. The hospital was rebuilt entirely in 1702 and despite subsequent modernisation and expansion, still today provides an atmospheric memorial to the charity of earlier times.

24 This Papal Bull of 1390 from Pope Boniface granted permission to Trinity Hospital to hold services 'and to have a bell in the same hospital'.

to attend mass and to say fifty aves and paternosters four times a day, and to remember the benefactors in their daily prayers.

De Vaux College was founded by Bishop Giles de Bridport in 1261-2 for 20 'poor, needy, honour-

able and teachable scholars' living there and studying theology and arts. Scholars had left Oxford following a series of arguments and visitations of plague during the 13th century and migrated to other centres within England and beyond. Salisbury had already gained an academic reputation under the influence of Bishop Poore who attracted a group of learned scholars to membership of the Chapter. It is likely that Bishop Bridport established his college to bring together a pre-existing informal community of masters and scholars. Most of the individuals who can be identified were from the local diocese, and more than half obtained degrees, increasingly in law rather than theology in contrast to the original intentions of the foundation. It is not surprising to learn that these young men did not always behave in a seemly manner; they were described as 'troublesome and rebellious' in 1319. But such comments were rare; in 1397 the college was 'well and honourably placed and governed in spiritualities, in temporalities and in persons'.

The early charters make no mention of any form of municipal organisation for the new town, but transactions in the Bishop's Court and conveyances of property suggest officials – a mayor, reeves, coroners and a bailiff – were regularly operating before the end of the 13th century. This was confirmed in 1306 when the relative status, duties and responsibilities of the bishop and city officials were clarified. The city was divided into four wards each represented by an elected alderman and used as administrative units for tax assessment and collection. The corporation consisted of interlocking groups – the 48 who were appointed from among the citizens admitted to the guild merchant, the 24 who were co-opted from the 48, and officials who were elected from the twenty-four.

The business debated by these citizens concerned the government and defence of the city, regulation of industry and trade, and the management of property owned by the corporation. Growing lists of such assets appeared in the city records, and it was found necessary to appoint a chamberlain with responsibility for rents and repairs. Amongst those described in the early 15th century were such desirable properties as 'another cottage there which

WILLIAM RUSSEL'S HOUSE, QUEEN STREET, SALISBURY

25   The interior of William Russel's House, Queen Street. Part of Watsons china and glass shop and owned by the Annetts family, this house is the oldest datable timber-framed building in Salisbury. A deed of 1306 gave William Russel, a wool merchant, a piece of land 39 ft. long with permission to build a house. Not discovered until 1975, it is a remarkably well preserved medieval structure.

Nicholas Shawe weaver holds with a garden adjacent pays yearly 10s'. Consistent with the policy of keeping noxious activities on the outskirts of the city itself was 'a building by the common latrine above Fisherton Bridge which Thomas Artour, skinner, holds, £1'.

It was necessary to send what would now be described as 'sweeteners' to higher officials; in the mayor's accounts of 1404-5 was 'a pipe of wine sent by agreement to John Bysle, knight, Sheriff of Wiltshire, for his kindnesses to the city in various matters £4'. The city had to pay the expenses of their two representatives when they attended Parliament and was, from time to time, required to subscribe to the defence of the realm – in 1404-5, £4 13s. 4d. paid the wages of 20 archers sent to the king in Wales. The gathering of troops prior to crossing the Channel with Henry V to fight the French in 1415 caused local disturbances when 'a crowd of the Earl of Lancaster's men who were lodged at Fisherton … attacked many of the city's men … killing four of them with arrows'. The corporation set additional watches and bore the cost of burying the men who died. Other officials such as ale-tasters and minstrels were appointed, but warranted little discussion as their roles raised no

26 *Salisbury Market Place from an 1877 guide book. In 1361 it was finally settled that Salisbury markets days would be on Tuesdays and Saturdays – as they still are. When the city's street plan was laid out a large space was left bounded by Blue Boar Row, Queen Street, New Canal and the river Avon.*

questions of jurisdiction and needed little expenditure.

A market had been held from the earliest days of the city's occupation. The bishop paid an annual fee of one palfrey to the king from 1219 to hold a market on Fridays and the charter of 1227 included the right to a weekly market on Tuesdays. Complaints came from nearby Wilton and the remaining community at Old Sarum of markets taking away their trade, but a Saturday market was also permitted in 1315. The first market stalls were probably put up in the area near St Thomas's church. Different parts of the Market Place were allocated for particular goods as it made commercial sense for sellers of similar commodities to be located together, and this arrangement also simplified the regulation of the market.

The activities of buying and selling were closely controlled to prevent obstructions and nuisances, and to protect consumers from unfair practices. In October 1401 John Saylere, baker, was fined four shillings and put in the pillory for two nights for selling underweight bread. Forestalling – purchasing goods from people on the road to Salisbury before

they reached the market – and regrating – buying in the market and then reselling at a higher price – were expressly forbidden in 1306. Trading started after sunrise, and for the first hour the servants of the bishop and canons had priority, after which the market was open to all. Perishables such as fish and meat could not be kept for sale on another day, so bargains might be had in the evening. Butchers were subject to many restrictions, for example they were required to slaughter their animals to the rear of Butcher Row and 'they should not carry about the foul parts or intestines of their beasts by day but by night'.

Gradually the market stalls became more permanent, at first remaining erected from week to week, later being replaced by open-fronted shops and workshops with living accommodation above; there is evidence of permanent structures in the fysschamels by the early 14th century and existing buildings in the market area can be dated to the 15th century. So the streets intruded upon the allocated market area which had, by the 17th century, shrunk to the space known today.

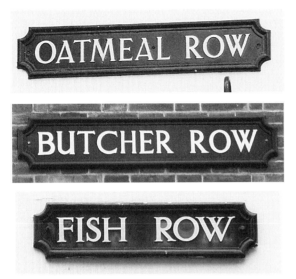

There were four market crosses in the city, each providing focus for a special trade. The Poultry Cross is the only survivor; some structure was there in 1307, and a 'new cross' is mentioned in 1448. It was 'repaired and beautified' in 1711. Despite its later name, fruit and vegetables were sold here at first as the original poultry market was in Silver Street. A cross was the central feature of the Cheesemarket on the north-western corner of the Market Place, also said to be newly built in the 1440s. Fruit and vegetables were sold there as well as dairy products. Amongst non-food items, wool was to become the key to medieval Salisbury's prosperity. The Yarn Market was another stone cross, sometimes known as the Wool Cross, providing a venue for local sales. Nearby was the official weigh-beam for judging the

27 *Street names came into common use which indicated the trade which took place there – le Bocherie, Otemele Corner, le Cookerowe.*

28 *The Poultry Cross about 1900. The present building is the result of the 19th-century reconstruction with subsequent restoration.*

29   Sheep and other animals were sold in the Market Place until the 1950s.

correct weight of sacks of wool. The fourth cross was situated some distance from the Market Place, to the south. Bernewelle or, later, Barnard's Cross was the site of the cattle market in the 15th century and was still there in the 17th century. When John Bremle was mayor in 1427 it was required that 'all beasts to be sold shall be kept in their proper place near Barnwell's Cross and Culver Street'.

By the early 19th century cattle were being sold with other commodities in the Market Place, and trading remained there until the 1950s. A purpose-built cattle market was opened in Scamell's Road in 1959. In 1996 it moved further out of the city centre to Netherhampton. Market trading was not the only use made of the crosses. Crowds gathered to hear friars preaching or political hustings, assignations were made, and they were useful for directing a stranger around the streets. Crowds also came to Salisbury for the fairs, which were important occasions from the earliest days of the city. At times there were as many as four, each with its special purpose; for example, the October fair sold hops, onions and cheese in the 18th century.

III

Growth and Prosperity

SALISBURY WAS BY FAR the most successful of the medieval new towns. It was forward-looking, not tied by tradition and, above all, prosperous. It has recently been described as the 'Milton Keynes of the Middle Ages' and by the 15th century it was clearly a boom town, its wealth based on wool and woollen cloth.

The growth of the city's population was linked to its expansion as a trading centre. The local population figures are intriguing because they contradict national trends. While the Black Death and successive outbreaks of the plague between 1348 and the early 16th century reduced the national population by over one third, Salisbury's population entered a period of rapid expansion. With its damp, low-lying situation and water channels, Salisbury is unlikely to have escaped the Black Death, but little is known of its impact here. Indeed, during this difficult period Salisbury was attracting immigrants from the surrounding countryside and fast becoming one of the great industrial centres in England. Population figures before the first census of 1801 are inevitably estimates and in the 14th and 15th centuries they are even more opaque, being largely based on tax returns, but Salisbury's population in 1400 was between 4,000 and 5,000 and by the mid-15th

30 *No. 91 Crane Street is a rare example of house improvement in Salisbury in the late 16th or early 17th century. Relatively few new houses were built in the city during this time.*

century it had grown to possibly 7 or 8,000. At a time when 3,000 was considered large, this placed it in the top six or seven cities in the country and even as high as fifth, the equivalent of a Manchester of today. After this Salisbury's population entered a period of stagnation and failed to prosper in the 16th and early 17th centuries, the classic period of expansion in the country as a whole. This atypical pattern can be explained by examining the growth and decline in Salisbury's woollen cloth industry.

In the late 13th and early 14th centuries, Salisbury and the surrounding area were better known for raw wool. There developed a substantial

31 Old Wiltshire horned sheep. Sheep grazed in enormous numbers on Salisbury Plain. Wool was the commodity which linked England closely to industrial cities like Bruges and Ghent where the finest textiles were made.

export trade through Southampton, and other south coast ports, for wool from the Plain which was collected in Salisbury. Teams of packhorses set off over Pepperbox Hill binding the economic fortunes of Wiltshire with those of Europe. From the late 14th century, however, English exports of raw wool were taxed heavily to finance Edward III's wars. At the same time, the Flemish cloth industry collapsed; English woollen cloth could, therefore, find a ready market on the Continent, so that in the 15th century exports of cloth replaced those of raw wool.

One of the reasons for the move to New Sarum was the plentiful water supply, which was ideal for the development of the cloth industry. As a new town, there were no tight guild regulations to hamper development and with its natural advantages it was

able to develop into a great industrial centre. At the height of Salisbury's prosperity, 50-60 per cent of the city's workforce was engaged in cloth making. The town produced a middle range cloth of one main colour with stripes of other colours woven into it. Known as 'striped rays', it sold for 1s. to 1s. 6d. a yard and was bought for servants in livery at Winchester College, while the scholars dressed in plain white gowns. London prostitutes apparently wore blue and yellow hoods made from Salisbury

are synonymous with Salisbury's prosperity at this time. These merchants traded mainly through Southampton and also Poole and Lymington, importing a huge variety of goods in exchange for woollen cloth. The Southampton Brokage Books of 1443-4 record the daily trade passing through the Bar Gates. The trade to Salisbury was the biggest part of Southampton's overland commerce in both volume and frequency. The chief commodity was

32 *(above) The streets would have been full of the smells and sounds of industry, the whirring of spinning wheels and the clanking of looms. The Green-croft, on slightly higher land, housed tenter frames for stretching the cloth, while the dyers' vats may well have been located by the River Avon, behind the Cheesemarket and Castle Street.*

33 *(left) Harnham Mill was one of several fulling mills around the edge of the city. Others were at Ford, Milford and Stratford-sub-Castle.*

34 *One of the rare stone buildings in the city, with walls of ashlar and flint, John Halle's hall was built in the 1460s and 1470s at right angles to New Canal and alongside a courtyard.*

rays, and the 'common prostitutes (who) shall have their house in Culver Street and not elsewhere under the penalty of imprisonment' also wore striped hoods of Salisbury cloth, suggesting that the city had at least one official brothel.

At the pinnacle of the city's organisation of the cloth industry stood the great merchants. Capitalists of the 15th century, powerful entrepreneurs and men of enormous wealth, their names – John Halle, William Swayne, John a Porte, William Lightfoot –

35 *The grand interior of John Halle's hall, with its timber-framed roof, 15th-century stone fireplace with his shield arms, merchant's mark and the stained glass, portray the affluence and style of one of Salisbury's leading citizens. The banqueting hall was restored by Pugin in 1834.*

36 *Ward list 1399-1400. Salisbury is fortunate in having documentary evidence of individual ordinary citizens at the end of the 14th century in the form of a list of residents in the four wards. Its purpose is unknown, but about one-fifth of the names include occupations on an apparently random basis. Several dyers are listed including John Bullok and John Murlawe.*

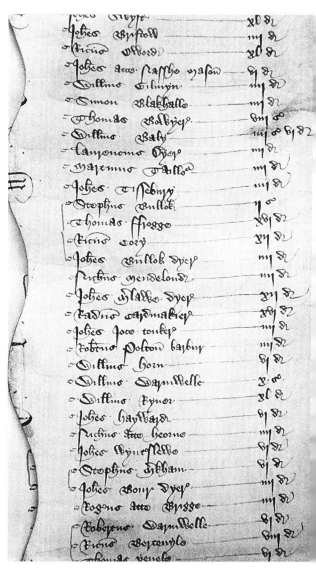

woad, the blue dye needed for the cloth industry. Dry French and Italian wines were very popular but occasionally sweet Malmsey wine was also imported. John Halle possessed a light ship, a caravel, the *James of Poole*, in which he carried vast quantities of salmon, herring, garlic, almonds, fruit and fine white soap, as well as the more mundane iron, tar, madder (a red dye) and alum (a mordant for fixing dyes). Such imports reflected the standard of living of some of the wealthier merchants as well as their trading

interests. Halle's shop, the 'Doggehole', was a veritable cornucopia of fashionable accessories and luxuries, selling hats, caps, haberdashery and huge amounts of spices. John Halle and William Swayne both owned numerous properties in the city; in 1455, Halle had 16 tenements or shops and Swayne twenty-three. Little is known of their background but each was essentially 'nouveau riche'. The hall of John Halle, the foyer of the present Odeon Cinema, reflects his success as a wool merchant.

Although more than half of Salisbury's population was engaged in occupations in or dependent on the textile industry, there were many other tradespeople exercising their skills in, for example, leather, wood, stone and metal. Those involved in the metal trades in Salisbury worked in gold, brass, iron, pewter and lead. These were highly skilled craftsmen creating products ranging from pins to jewellery, scissors and church bells. Smiths were an essential part of any economy based on horse power, and they also contributed to vehicle manufacture, building and tool-making for many other trades. As the centre of a large diocese Salisbury was the natural focus for a bell-founding industry, bells were made here from the 14th to the 17th centuries and supplied to churches in neighbouring counties. Although not all medieval bells were marked with their maker's name, one known Salisbury maker was John Barbur, who died in 1404; he lived in Winchester Street and described himself as a brasier, or worker in brass, though he also worked in copper and made other moulded metalware as well as bells. His will listed the tools and products of his trade, made extensive bequests to the churches and religious orders of the city and ordered sixty pairs of shoes to be distributed to the poor and needy.

While much of the food consumed by the citizens was grown in the surrounding area and bought in the market, and preparation was done by each household, processing by butchers, bakers and brewers was important. Ale was a universal drink before the arrival of coffee and tea; in 1464 an agreement was reached between the corporation and the bishop as to prices and quality, decided by four tasters representing the wards of the city. The best would be sold for 1d. a flagon (1.5 gallons), three times the price of a lower quality brew.

It is not only in recent times that visitors have been important to the economy of Salisbury. Inns to accommodate and feed strangers were amongst the early establishments in the city. The cathedral

37   Salisbury craftsmen have worked in leather for many centuries. Harry Till was photographed in May 1945 making a saddle in his Brown Street shop.

itself had always been an attraction, significantly enhanced following the canonisation of St Osmund in 1457. Amongst the miracles reputed to result from his intervention was the recovery of a child from drowning. Apparently dead, it was placed on Osmund's tomb, then opened its eyes and smiled. Numerous royal visits, including four from Henry VII in eight years, both to the city itself and to the nearby royal palace at Clarendon, brought the monarch's entourage to patronise the city's facilities, and also demanded conspicuous consumption by the leading citizens for new matching gowns and headgear in red and green.

The substantial households of the Close depended on the tradespeople of the city for supplies. They were given priority for food marketing, and fuel, candles, oil, soap, pots and furnishings were also

*38 Pilgrim's badge of Thomas Becket
found in Salisbury's drainage collection.
Such items were collected as souvenirs
after a pilgrimage. St Osmund's shrine
drew pilgrims in large numbers.*

regular requirements. They were employers of many
servants and other lay workers. The barber employed
for the choristers was paid 6s. 8d. a year, and the
laundress 10s., for which she did the washing for 16
people! Uniform livery for the choristers and vicars
choral provided custom to local drapers. The
choristers wore blue; in the mid-15th century two
bales of cloth worth £4 were purchased and the
tailor was paid 13s. 4d. for making robes for 14
choristers and the sub-magister. Taverns were
frequented by the young clergy, against the rules of
their calling, to the extent that a curfew was
introduced in 1414 closing the High Street Gate at
8 p.m. in winter and 9 p.m. in summer, the other
gates an hour earlier in each case. There were many
occasions when these men were caught climbing
the wall to return from a drinking session or from a
visit to a prostitute.

Salisbury's original guild merchant was
established in 1306 and included all the merchants
and townsmen of importance in the city – over 200
people. Known as the Guild of St George, this

organisation was not divided by craft and was perhaps
similar to a modern Chamber of Commerce. The
government of the town and its trade were so
interlocked that it is often difficult to distinguish
one from the other. Hence the town hall and the
guildhall were synonymous up to the 15th century
and both bodies met in the original Bishop's
Guildhall, on the site of the present Guildhall in the
Market Place. Little is known of the activities of the
guild merchant and of its relationship with the later
craft guilds.

As industry developed, workers and craftsmen
of each separate trade congregated together in, for
example, Silver Street, Ironmonger Row and Pot
Row, and organised themselves for mutual protection
against competitors, leading to the formation of craft
guilds. The earliest reference in Salisbury is to the
skinners in 1380, but by the 15th century many guilds
were clearly firmly established. In 1415, before the
Battle of Agincourt, the guilds were asked to
contribute money, 'hobblers, archers, and other
defensible men', as demanded by Henry V. They
joined the king's forces in Salisbury bound for
Southampton and so to Harfleur and victory in
France. A ledger of September 1440 lists 38 trades
whose members were to construct a large ditch
around the city. This list shows that trades like the
tailors, weavers, fullers and butchers had their own

*39 (top left)   In 1458 the house opposite the Poultry Cross was
left to Trinity Hospital by John Winchester, a barber surgeon. To
improve their own expertise, the surgeons had permission from the
mayor and justices to 'have the body of any executed felon to make
an anatomy thereof'.*

*40 (top right)   The Joiners' Guildhall in St Ann's Street dates
from the early 17th century. The fine façade has elaborate carved
work with six grotesque timber corbels. Possibly the work of Humphrey
Beckham, Chamberlain and Warden of the Joiners' Company, it
displays a very high standard of craftsmanship.*

*41 (bottom)   The Pheasant Inn and Shoemakers' Guildhall in
about 1910. In 1638, Philip Crew, schoolmaster and son of a
shoemaker, left his house to the Shoemakers' Company, stating in
his will, that members should 'inlardge … my said Dwellinge house
… and make the same fitt for a hall for the said Company'.*

guild. Some, like the carpenters, included several different trades, such as fletchers (arrow makers) and bow makers, but each trade was distinctive and those who made bows could not provide the arrows or even the strings for them.

Craft guilds protected the interests of their members and their customers and maintained quality through a strict apprenticeship training and by excluding strangers from the town. For example, in 1479 the tailors stated that 'no apprentice should be taken for less than seven years … no body could set up shop without the sanction of the guild wardens'. The rules of the barber surgeons forbade unskilled people 'to take or meddle with any cure for chirurgery'. Guilds had both religious and social functions; each had its own priest and often its own hall. Two which survive today are the Joiners' Hall and the Shoemakers' Guildhall, both dating from the 17th century. The provision of welfare benefits was an important service. Members paid into a common box which helped the sick or those who had suffered industrial accident. Funeral expenses were covered for guild members and pensions given to widows.

Few women entered the structured world of the guilds, though there are examples of girls being formally apprenticed and married women assisting in their husbands' businesses. Widows were permitted to continue to trade in their late husband's place until they remarried. Seventeenth-century records mention solitary women among merchants, tanners, butchers, pewterers, tailors, glovers and maltsters.

Guild Charters exist for the two largest guilds, the weavers and the tailors. The weavers were a powerful guild owning considerable property in the city. A ledger of 1420 shows that 81 master weavers and 207 journeyman weavers attended a council meeting. They worshipped in St Edmund's church and were buried there. In 1415, Alice, wife of Thomas Hamme, 'desires to be buried in the Church of Seynte Edmund's opposite the altar … where the light of the weavers remains'. Dating from the early 15th

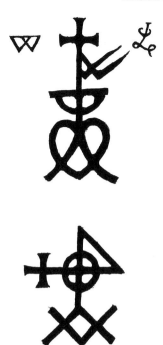

42 *The merchants' marks of William Lightfoot and William Swayne. Rich merchants paid for the enlargements on the south side of the chancel of St Thomas's church, thereby advertising their wealth. One pillar has the inscription 'John Nichol, the founder of this peler'.*

century, all seven ledgers of the Tailors' Guild survive. The conspicuous wealth of the tailors was revealed when the chancel of St Thomas's church collapsed in 1448. The cost of rebuilding was shared between the Dean and Chapter, who rebuilt the north side, and the merchants and wealthy citizens. William Swayne was the patron and friend of the Tailors' Guild and built, at his own expense, the lovely lady chapel for his family and the guild. Lettering painted on the main roof beams of the chapel asks for prayers for the souls of William Swayne and Chrystian, his wife.

The tailors also presented their own pageant. The guild owned the Giant, known in the Middle Ages as St Christopher, once 14 feet tall and unique in the country, having survived the Reformation. Though his origins are unknown, the earliest

43 *'Hob-nob', with his snapping jaws, cleared the way for the Giant in procession and chased apprentices into the open water channels if they hurled unpleasant missiles at him. The Giant was also accompanied by six Morris men and two whifflers, one carrying a mace, the other an enormous wooden sword, as can be seen in this photograph of 1887.*

reference was in 1570 when Gregory Clark promised 'to fynde and sett goinge for the accustomed pageant of Mydsomer feaste, the Gyant, the three black boyes, the bearer of the Gyant and one person to play the Divill's part'. The devil may well have been played by Hob-nob, the hobby horse, and the Giant's companion in their present home in Salisbury Museum.

Festival days were celebrated with processions and feasting and the Giant appeared in most: St George's Day, St Osmund's Day and, above all, the festival of the Tailors' Guild which was celebrated on Midsummer's Eve, the eve of St John the Baptist. The Giant left his home in the Tailors' Hall, on the north side of Milford Street, and processed round the town to the cathedral, accompanied by the mayor and council and representatives from the guilds on horseback, with the tailors at the front. Celebrations continued throughout the next day with further drinking and feasting 'in the most godly wise'. At a time of widespread disease and uncertainty, these lavish celebrations must have provided relief from the tribulations of day to day living. By 1611, Puritan attitudes were enforced in the city and the wardens of the Tailors' Guild were sent to prison for patronising Morris dances on Sunday.

In 1612, James I gave the city a new charter which finally freed the corporation from the bishop's control. The craft guilds were reorganised as trade companies with distinct regulations laid down by the town council. But the weavers and tailors kept their independent organisation, and in practice the situation appears to have changed little. New orders of 1622 forbade the bakers from making anything but plain bread except for Good Friday, Christmas and funerals. They were not to make or sell 'bread made with butter or milk, spice cakes, buns, biscuits … upon pain to forfeit for every default ten shillings'; these delicacies were reserved for the company of cooks. The butchers, in 1614, had equally strict rules covering apprenticeship and the control of 'forraine butchers', as well as hygiene and consumer protection. Bulls were beaten at the bull ring, which was fixed in the Market Place until 1835, the rule being that they should be beaten the day before they were slaughtered because that made the flesh more tender and digestible to eat!

The council took an active interest in the companies in the 17th century, excluding strangers and restraining traders from setting up in Fisherton, Milford, Harnham and the Close. By 1700, however, the trade companies were struggling against competition from non-members. The tailors petitioned Parliament unsuccessfully in that year to ban those practising unlawfully in the city. Monopolistic practices had become obsolete and when, in 1786, the Salisbury Commercial Company was founded 'to protect and promote the general trading interests of the city', the craft guilds were finally dead.

Politics and commerce were closely intertwined in medieval Salisbury. The wealthy wool merchants were also men of influence and power in the city. John Halle and William Swayne were each mayor several times in the 1450s and 1460s and Salisbury's M.P. Halle was reputedly an arrogant and aggressive man; William Swayne was equally forthright and the two protagonists disrupted meetings to such an extent that the bishop and council met in special session to discuss their behaviour. It was decreed that if 'William Swayne or John Halle shall again offend … they are to be fined twenty shillings for the benefit of the city; if a second time, forty shillings: and a third time to be imprisoned'. An example of their 'malicious and unbecoming speeches' is recorded: 'I defy thee; what art thou? … I am as rich as thou, and greater beloved than thou.'

During the late 15th century the struggle between the citizens and the bishop, of which this was a part, reached its climax. The bishop was the feudal overlord of the city. He had responsibility for settling land ownership disputes and the right to take tallage, an arbitrary tax, whenever the king did so from his own lands. As the citizens grew wealthier they wanted freedom and self-government. Real friction had occurred in 1302 when the citizens refused to pay tallage. They took their case to the King in Council and were given a choice: either pay no taxes but receive no privileges, as under the 1227 Charter, or keep their rights and pay the tallage. In

44 *The High Street Gate from the Close, showing Norman stonework. Edward III granted the Dean and Chapter permission to surround the Close with an 'embattled wall of stone and to hold it so enclosed to themselves and their successors'. The gate once had a portcullis as additional defence against the town and the gates are still shut nightly.*

45 *The stone for the Close wall came, with royal permission, from the Norman cathedral at Old Sarum and many of the carved stones can still be seen, particularly in Exeter Street.*

1305, the mayor and council surrendered all their privileges and chose to pay no taxes to the bishop. It was a disastrous decision. Without protection, trade declined and a year later the citizens gave in and their privileges, and their taxes, were restored in a new charter which emphasised the subordinate position of the mayor. The Close wall, begun in 1327, helped to safeguard the bishop and his canons from the increasingly ambitious citizens. Resentment continued, coupled with frustration that the profits from the markets and fairs went to the bishop. In 1395, the citizens again lost a dispute and had to promise obedience.

The contest reached new heights, with nine years of litigation, in the 1460s and '70s. Powerful men were in conflict: the strong-headed John Halle on one side and his great rival William Swayne, supported by the very influential Bishop Beauchamp,

46   No. 49 New Canal. John Buterlegh, wool merchant and mayor in the 1380s, was amongst the eight citizens who appeared in a dispute before the king. This is one of his three 14th-century properties which can be traced today. The cusped barge boards are the only surviving examples of a once common feature.

conflict ensued. Both the bishop and citizens presented petitions to Edward IV. The bishop accused Halle of defying his authority. Halle retaliated by demanding jurisdiction over the city in return for rent, leaving the bishop in control of just the Close. The bishop appeared in person before the king demanding that another mayor be chosen 'of sad, sober and discrete disposition'.

John Halle did his cause no good, was insolent to both the bishop and the king, and was imprisoned, possibly in the Tower of London, but the council refused to replace him and by 1466 he was released and reinstated. Later that year he organised the welcome for King Edward IV when he visited Salisbury. In the end the bishop strengthened his position when, in 1474, future mayors had to take an oath acknowledging the overlordship of the bishop, promising 'to serve him well'. In the 15th century, then, despite the new power of the city based on its wealth, the bishop could still be sure of the king's support. Not until the 1612 Charter were the citizens finally emancipated.

on the other. This controversy arose over the ownership of a piece of land in St Thomas's church-yard. Swayne had completed the Lady Chapel and had obtained from the bishop a plot of unoccupied land to build a house for his chantry priest. When, in 1464, the building was at least partly built 'so that the walls and chimneys were of good height', Halle, as mayor, claimed that the land belonged to the corporation. He ordered that the building be pulled down and the workmen imprisoned. Although Halle's claim appears to have been weak, a bitter

47   A possible representation of John Halle in the stained glass, John Halle's banqueting hall. Hatcher described Halle as a 'turbulent demagogue' who 'even in the royal presence was guilty of violent language and impropriety of deportment'.

IV

New Ideas and Challenges

FOR A CITY WHICH OWED its very existence to the church, the religious changes of the 16th century were traumatic. As the cathedral was not a monastic foundation, it was saved from the worst rigours of the legislation which brought about the 'dissolution of the monasteries', but it did suffer severely from the alterations in practice which were required. In 1539 the destruction of St Osmund's shrine took 52 days, suggesting the great care with which the elaborately decorated and bejewelled edifice was dismantled. With it went the celebrations and pageantry associated with St Osmund's Eve, which had been a highlight of the city's year. Cathedral plate worth 2000 marks was sent to the King's Mint at Bristol in 1549, and there were later sales of more plate, ornaments and copes. Many illuminated manuscripts were removed from the library, though fortunately some survived.

A significant feature of the medieval church had been the establishment of chantries to protect the memory of their benefactors. *Valor Ecclesiasticus* in 1535 named ten in Salisbury, served by 13 chantry chaplains, with a total estimated value of £98 5s. 11d. That of Bishop Bridport dated back to the 13th century, though his chaplain was the poorest, paid only £3 6s. 8d. a year. All were closed down in 1547 and masses were no longer said for the souls of their founders. In the early 16th century there had been at least nine regular daily services in the cathedral; fifty years later there were only two. Cranmer's new *English Prayer Book* took the place of Osmund's *Use*

of Sarum, though the first edition of 1549 did include some elements of the old rites.

On the whole, Salisbury's bishops proved responsive to the opposing pressures under which they worked, though they did not always find it easy to take the chapter, canons and citizens with them. Lorenzo Campeggio, the only foreigner ever to hold the see, was appointed by Henry VIII and served as papal legate and Cromwell's assistant in the matter of the king's divorce but was removed from the bishopric in 1534 for absenteeism. His successor Shaxton was a fervent Protestant who, two years after his appointment, wrote to Cromwell that the people of Salisbury called him a heretic and would see him hanged. Despite his efforts, he fell foul of authority and landed temporarily in the Tower. Bishop Salcot

48 *An occupant of Hemingsby in the early 16th century was Canon Edward Powell, who acted as advocate for Catherine of Aragon during Henry VIII's divorce, and was hung, drawn and quartered for his pains.*

49 *Fisherton Anger Church was demolished in 1852. The three Protestants were examined in the church before being condemned. Maundrel is reputed to have declared, 'wooden images were good to rost a Sholder of mutton, but evill in the Church'.*

50 *Plaque to the three Protestant martyrs.*

THREE PROTESTANT MARTYRS
THIS TABLET COMMEMORATES THE DEATHS
IN SALISBURY OF
WILLIAM COBERLEY
JOHN MAUNDREL
JOHN SPICER
WHO, ON THE 24th DAY OF MARCH, 1556,
YIELDED THEIR BODIES TO THE FLAMES
RATHER THAN DENY TRUTHS RECORDED IN
"THE SCRIPTURE OF TRUTH" (DANIEL 10 21)
"THEY OVERCAME THE ACCUSER BY THE
BLOOD OF THE LAMB, AND BY THE WORD
OF THEIR TESTIMONY; AND THEY LOVED
NOT THEIR LIVES UNTO THE DEATH"
(REVELATION 12 11)

'alias Capon' held the see from 1539 to 1557, when changes under three monarchs required great flexibility which he exhibited with such skill that an early 20th-century historian of Salisbury wrote, 'it is not easy to say anything good of him'. The return to Catholicism under Queen Mary was resented by many and resisted openly by the brave. Amongst the Protestant martyrs was John Maundrel, who was burnt at the stake in March 1556 at Fisherton. Maundrel a farmer, Spicer a mason, and Coberly a tailor were tried for heresy before Salcot and condemned to death.

Salisbury had no bishop for three years after Salcot's death. John Jewel was appointed in 1560 and faced the difficult task of establishing the Elizabethan church in a diocese heavily in debt, with buildings in disrepair and clergy who neglected to say services and were accused of drunkenness and womanising.

51 *Aula le Stage still has a 13th-century core. It was extensively restored in the 16th century with ceilings resembling those at Hampton Court Palace. During the same century the Close first became a desirable address for wealthy citizens.*

52 *De Vaux College was dissolved in 1542. The scholars had already returned to Oxford or left for other universities, so only the chaplains and stewards remained at its closure.*

Worse than that, Canon Bilson was condemned to the pillory in London for 'sorcery and magick and curious and forbidden arts'. The general decay was symbolised by the damage done when the spire was struck by lightning during a great storm the previous year. Jewel was an efficient administrator who conscientiously visited all corners of the widespread region, but he is remembered more for his decree to remove 'idolatrous' medieval stained glass windows. His insistence that the canons be in residence and take responsibility for repairs to their houses improved the condition of the Close, and the novelty of wives and families for married clergy changed the nature of households here. Some new houses and a shop were built, and tenants included varied tradespeople, especially around the North Gate.

Outside the Close walls other religious foundations also suffered at this time. Both Dominican and Franciscan Friaries surrendered in October 1538. The former had been found 'in good order' earlier in the year, but gained only a brief respite. Their debts amounted to £80 and their assets only a little property, their garden, some silver and

53   *St Thomas's church has one of the largest surviving wall paintings of the Last Judgement. In 1593, the Doom painting 'disappeared' when Gusset was paid 22s. for 'washinge the Church with lyme'.*

fishing rights on the River Avon. Some of the Franciscans' property was sold for £14 2s. to offset debts of £19 owing for food and drink. Charles Bulkeley offered £100 for the building, saying he had lodged there for 20 years and his rent of 26s. 8d. was the only regular income of the friars. De Vaux College was assessed in 1535 with an annual income of £94 15s.; it was dissolved in 1542. Because much of its income came from benefactions it suffered the same fate as the chantries. Similarly vulnerable was St John's Chapel on Harnham Bridge, but its association with the Hospital of St Nicholas, protected by the powerful patronage of the Earl of Pembroke, ensured its survival. Trinity Hospital, too, continued to care for the poor, unaffected by the upheavals elsewhere.

54 *St Thomas's church without the Doom painting. In 1593, Roger Lovell was paid £8 18d. for 'making of the Queenes Armes' with its Tudor dragon supporter. This was placed over the chancel arch until the Doom painting was restored in 1881.*

The College of St Edmund was closed in 1546 and its property sold to William St Barbe for £400, but the church remained, with St Thomas's and St Martin's, to serve the parishioners of the city. But here too there is evidence of the changes imposed on practices and fabric. At St Edmund's in 1550, 10s. 4d. was paid 'to masons for pullying downe of the hygh Auter'. Three years later the change of monarch was recorded when 7d. was spent on 'ryngegyng the xxi day of July when oʳ Souerenge lady mary quene was proclaymed', 3s. 4d. for 'settyng up of the Awter' and other payments to re-equip the church. In 1560 'latyn bookes' had to be submitted to the cathedral and a new communion book was purchased, as well as 2d. for 'holly agaynst crystmas'.

The ordinary citizens of Salisbury might have wondered at the comings and goings of altars, statues and plate, and at their familiar services changing from Latin to English. They would have missed the annual pageantry associated with St Osmund's Day in July, and with many of the guild chantries which also had property confiscated, though the Tailors' Guild retained its midsummer feast and procession. In 1578 it became a crime not to go to church.

The church was solely responsible for education until the 16th century. The medieval cathedral provided two schools: the Song School which taught reading and writing as well as music, and the Grammar School which taught Latin. The latter was located just outside St Ann's Gate. The numbers of students, both boys and older clerics, caused some discipline problems and disputes as to responsibility for their order. Masters were employed and funds devoted to the Grammar School until the middle of the 15th century. By 1540, the Chancellor's Grammar School had been refounded inside the Close and there appears to have been no school in the town. In the mid-1540s a plea was sent to the king saying that 'the Cytye of Newe Sarum is a goodly Cytye and well peopled, as is well-known, full of youth' and asking that he 'appoynt a Scole mayster there for the Inducement of youth'. Edward VI founded many grammar schools and his visit to Salisbury in 1551 may have stimulated developments here. Christopher Benett was appointed to 'the office of Schoolemaster of the Free Schoole to be kept within the precincts of the Close'. His successor in 1563

reason was the long-established guilds which were interested in stability and order, not progress, and meant the city failed to respond to the changing needs of the market. The demand in the first half of the 16th century was for high quality undyed broadcloths and Salisbury continued to produce the

55   *Cathedral choristers attended their grammar school in what is now known as Wren Hall. The schoolroom was part of William Braybroke's canonry, adjoining the master's house.*

was told 'that he should keep this school like a free school and common Grammar School and refuse no fit boy'. Braybroke House was allocated as the residence for the master, which arrangement continued into the 20th century.

Fluctuations in economic prosperity were felt by the people in Salisbury, as elsewhere. It is difficult to establish exactly why the town declined as a great woollen cloth centre but the Southampton Brokage Books show a considerable downturn in the Salisbury trade by the 1520s and 1530s. Possibly the main

cheaper striped rays. A few of the city's great wool merchants survived into the 16th century, including William Webbe who left £100 to help the young tradesmen of the city as well as the 'dye house by Water Lane with all tenements to the same apperteyning and ymplementes thereof', but by the 1570s only one Salisbury merchant was trading through Southampton and he went bankrupt.

Salisbury's decline was linked with that of Southampton as London took over the export trade. Some Salisbury merchants did switch to London but

56 *The Greencroft was used for walking, playing and for fairs, as well as for executions and burials.*

a combination of factors damaged Salisbury's economy and the city ceased to grow while other towns developed rapidly. In the 1520s Salisbury was possibly the seventh largest town in England; a century later, she had fallen to 16th in the population league table. It is important, however, not to exaggerate her demise as those employed in the woollen industry still far outnumbered any other occupation in Salisbury. Diversification came gradually as the clothiers turned to producing white broadcloths for the London market for export, thus

effecting a minor 'industrial revolution' in the city. Despite this belated reorganisation, Salisbury was no longer a boom town and the impact on the people is reflected by the building of the first workhouse. By the late 1620s, following a disastrous slump in the cloth trade, possibly over one third of the city was impoverished and needing relief.

Against this disturbed background, the city authorities extended their interest in the well-being of the people. The Greencroft open space was acquired by the city in the middle of the 16th century.

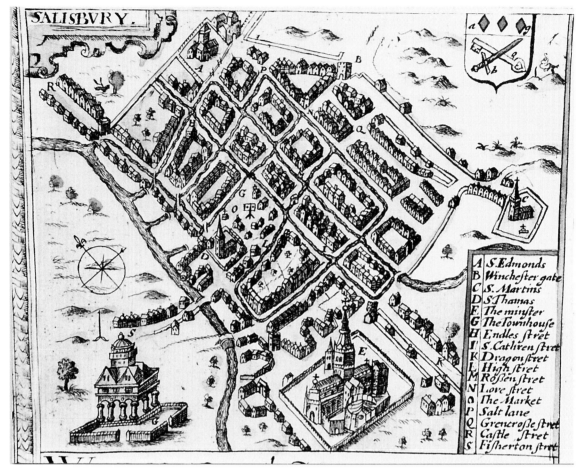

SALISBVRY.

A	S. Edmonds
B	Winchester gate
C	S. Martins
D	S. Thomas
E	The minster
G	The Townhouse
H	Endles stret
I	S. Cathren stret
K	Dragon stret
L	High stret
M	Rossen stret
N	Love stret
O	The Market
P	Salt lane
Q	Grencrosse stret
R	Castle stret
S	Fisherton stret

57   *The Council House, in the bottom left-hand corner of John Speed's map of 1611, dominated the eastern end of the Market Place for two hundred years.*

The 48 had decided, in 1565, to replace the medieval Council House, on the corner of St Thomas's churchyard, but the impressive new building was not begun until 1579 and completed in 1584. In 1562 a scavenger was appointed at £20 a year to carry out 'all suche myre, durt, dust and soyle' which the citizens had to make ready in tidy heaps and they were not to include stable dung or garden weeds. The council also ordered a survey of all the houses in the city in 1595 to search out overcrowding, which was considered a disease and fire risk. Harsh restric-tions were imposed on 'foreigners' who wished to live and work here.

Visitors, especially wealthy ones, were welcomed however. Queen Elizabeth came in 1584 and the King of Portugal in 1595. 'Divers noble personages' attended 'a race runned with horses at the Fursyes thre myles from Harnem Hyll' for which the major prize was a golden bell valued at £50. This took place in March 1583 and Salisbury Races continue to the present day.

V

Coping with Change

SALISBURY'S PROBLEMS in the 17th century were, in many respects, a microcosm of those in the country at large: poverty, plague, religious strife, civil war and witchcraft, all reflecting the uncertainty of the times. James I's new charter of 1612 should have enabled the city government to exercise more control. In practice, the organisation changed little for some time, but the declining prosperity meant that the city authorities' attempts to deal with growing unemployment and vagrancy produced a unique experiment in 17th-century Puritan philanthropy.

There are early references to a workhouse in Brown Street in 1396 but the first city workhouse or bridewell was built in 1564 in Winchester Street 'to hold or set to work idle people'. In 1602, a workhouse with 12 beds was built in St Thomas's churchyard. From the 1590s, bad harvests and prolonged economic depression led to widespread poverty, malnutrition and disease and the existing system was unable to cope. The rural poor came into Salisbury in search of work and relief, and between 1598 and 1638, 600 vagrants were whipped out of Salisbury – the whipping post was in the Market Place – and returned to the parish of their birth so that they would not be a burden on the city. Only locals were allowed to beg. Salisbury's register of passports for the early 17th century represents a unique record. The vagrants were given a passport and were checked by constables along their specified route home. Many were single women and some of the records reveal personal tragedies.

Crises were also caused by outbreaks of the plague. With its open water channels, Salisbury was a breeding ground for disease. Between 1563 and 1723 there were six major outbreaks in the city. In St Edmund's parish alone, there were 172 burials in one hot summer month in 1563, while in 1604, 1,190

58 *Portrait of Joan Popley. The workhouse was partly funded by rents from London properties given to the town by Joan Popley in 1570.*

59   *A beggar's. 'Agnes Jones,* alias *Symes, with her two children, was taken vagrant and wandering. She has been in Fisherton gaol for two years … and was freed at the Marleboroughe assizes and came back to this city. She was punished. Passport to Frome Sellwood, Som., where she was born and last dwelt; three days assigned.' From a register of passports, April 1605.*

people, approximately 17 per cent of the city's population, died. St Edmund's parish register in that year recorded that 'There died in the moneth of August in this parish A Hundred & twoe all these of the plague save only twoe.' Infected households had to be isolated, and those in quarantine too poor to sustain themselves were supported from public relief. During the 1620s, Salisbury's fragile economy suffered as poverty threatened to overwhelm the city. Bad harvests and contraction in both domestic and overseas markets for cloth brought the Wiltshire woollen industry to the brink of catastrophe. In the plague year of 1627, one third of the population of Salisbury was reported to be 'sick of the famine and many of them begin to look as green and pale as death'. Town life was disrupted, the rich fled, markets ceased to function and food shortages added to the

60   *Water channels in Castle Street. Visitors John Evelyn and Celia Fiennes wrote of dirty streets and 'negligently kept' water courses.*

misery of disease. Salisbury was described by John Taylor as being 'much overcharged with poore as having in three parishes neere 3000'.

The story of the 1627 plague in Salisbury is a remarkable one and owes its fame to John Ivie's *Declaration* of 1661 in which this prominent Puritan vividly recalled his work as mayor in the 1620s. Stringent precautions had been taken to prevent the plague reaching Salisbury from London. The Salisbury carrier, Morgan Morse, had to leave his goods well outside the city and wardens prevented strangers from entering. Nevertheless, the disease arrived in Salisbury in March 1627 and within four days many had fled, with 60 carts leaving the city daily. The cathedral clergy blockaded themselves in the Close and all cathedral services were suspended for 12 months. Only John Ivie remained in authority, assisted by two petty constables, and his household of two men and an old serving woman. With just £80 to deal with 3,000 desperate people, he worked rapidly knowing that his actions literally meant life or death. He levied the poor rate and organised storehouses stocked with essential items in the three parishes. A pest house in Bugmore was built for the worst cases.

The remaining citizens drowned their fears in drink. Ivie closed down 100 alehouses causing the animosity of the 'brewers … the innkeepers, all the drunkards, the whoremasters and lewd fellows'. One inn chose to disregard Ivie's directive and within three days all its occupants were dead. Ivie commented 'It pleased God to give me power to suppress all saving that one house; then the God of power did suppress that house in his own judgement'. His troubles were not quite over. 'A base woman', the widow Biby, set the pest house on fire and when Ivie arrived on the scene he found 87 'poor souls' sitting in the field, 'many of them almost naked and one quite naked'. The pest house was quickly rebuilt, the inmates re-clothed and surprisingly few died. By the winter of 1627, the plague had subsided; 369

61   *John Ivie's 'Declaration', 1661.*

62   *Wording of plaque to John Ivie in Salisbury Guildhall.*

> In lasting memory of
> John Ivie
> Goldsmith
> Mayor of the City of New Sarum
> in the year 1627
> when the City was sore stricken
> with plague
> so that many citizens fled
> for safety, leaving him to bear
> the burden of his office alone
> aided by two petty constables
> Christopher Brathart and John Pinhorn
> "You have done your country good service
> For which we are all beholden
> To God & you".

people had died in St Edmund's and St Thomas's parishes but without John Ivie's leadership the death rate would undoubtedly have been far higher.

To deal with the underlying poverty in the city, John Ivie and councillors Matthew Bee and Henry Sherfield produced an ambitious plan which involved three linked institutions. First, an enlarged workhouse was built in 1623 in St Thomas's churchyard which would not only be a house of correction for the 'lewder sort' but would prevent poverty by teaching poor children a trade, sending them to the homes of spinners and knitters in the town. Thus a basic cause of unemployment was tackled; in 1625, 100 children were being provided for in this way.

Second, a municipal brewery was established in 1623 in an attempt to intervene in a thriving sector of the town's economy. The profits were to help towards the relief of the poor, both in the workhouse and in the city generally, including apprenticeships

for children, and lead to a reduction in the poor rates. Salisbury brewers, however, organised a successful boycott. The initial loans were never paid off and the brewhouse was eventually closed in 1646 still owing £450.

The third aspect of the scheme was initiated by Ivie himself and was perhaps the most original. A storehouse was installed in Brown Street in 1628 to supply all that was necessary to maintain a minimum standard of living for the city's poor: bread, butter, cheese, beer and fuel, all at cost price. The Puritan ethic was preserved by granting tokens to the poor which could be exchanged for goods in the storehouse, rather than cash which could be squandered on drink. Like the brewery, the storehouse faced problems and could not cope with fluctuations in trade or extraordinary outbursts of sickness. A survey of two parishes in 1635 listed everyone in need of relief and showed that poverty

	Children	Age	Ability/Employment	Earning weekly	Relief weekly
Widow Cacksey		75	labour done		4d
John Nuby		46	wants work		2s
Dinah Nuby		36			
	John	16	sick abed		
	Robert	11	sick		
	William	9	quill	6d	
	Mary Rebecca	1			
John Butler		40	in gaol		
Avis uxor		35			1s 6d
	Crisse	14	bonelace	1s	
	Nabb	9			
	Ann	7			
	Thomas	3			
Mary Brakes		29	her husband gone from her	12d	6d
	John	5			
	Mary	2			
Thomas Underhill		66	weaver	3s	6d
Judith uxor		54	lame hand	10d	
	Eleanor	20	bonelace	14d	
	Elizabeth	16	spin	4d	
	Christian	7	school		
	Henry	5			

63 Extract adapted from a survey of the poor in St Edmund's and St Thomas's parishes in 1635.

64 *The courtyard of the workhouse in Crane Street. In the new workhouse, the regulations governing the poor were harsher and more conventional.*

was not the prerogative of those unable or unwilling to work. Some were sick or blind or, at 75 years of age, 'their labour done', but many were simply 'miserably poor' or 'wanted work'. By 1640 the storehouse was forced to close. Even the workhouse scheme needed to be modified because few employers were willing to train and effectively subsidise poor children. In 1637, the workhouse in St Thomas's was replaced by a larger building, now Church House, in Crane Street. Despite its ultimate failure, this Puritan scheme remains an interesting experiment in the alleviation of poverty which commands respect.

Salisbury escaped the worst excesses of the Civil War. It was never under siege and there were no major battles as at Newbury or Wardour. The city has been described as an 'open house', of no military value but where both sides could recoup and recover.

The citizens suffered because soldiers needed food and billets when garrisoned here. With its Puritan leanings, Salisbury supported Parliament although, like many cities, its true loyalties were divided, with the Dean and Chapter supporting the King and secretly arming themselves. Their influence in the town was considerable and they were given support by one of Salisbury's M.P.s, the ardent Royalist Robert Hyde. Philip, the fourth Earl of Pembroke, Parliament's commander for the Wessex region, delivered arms to the city, and the mayor formed a band of volunteers promising loyal support to Pembroke. It was a kind of 'phoney war' at first, with little more than skirmishes in the streets. In 1643 a Royalist force from Oxford, under Lord Hertford, passed through Salisbury on its way to Somerset. On various occasions, Royalist troops seem to have caused the kind of problems associated with bored mobs of young men. Two Salisbury craftsmen had reported the loss of their wives' petticoats and later the King's soldiers were seen dancing in the streets in these ladies' garments. In March 1644, the soldiers 'having cut holes in their hats and placed lighted candles in them … ran about the streets dancing and roaring'.

In 1644, Parliamentary troops under Edward Ludlow, retreating from Warminster, passed rapidly through the city pursued by Royalists. Some of the citizens publicly enjoyed the sight of this ungainly retreat but were to suffer later when Ludlow returned to fine all those 'who were disaffected in the town'. The city appeared trapped between the two contending armies, but conflict was averted when Parliament's army withdrew to Andover. In August, Parliamentary troops robbed the cathedral of crosses, pictures and silver plate. Their commander was forced to restrain them and the plate was returned, but not the 'superstitious relics'. According to tradition, repairs were secretly financed by the Royalist Hyde family.

In October 1644 the King himself arrived in Salisbury with his army, following victories in the

65 *Portrait of Edward Ludlow on horseback.*

West Country. He left cannon at Longford Castle to bolster its defences and his troops mustered at Clarendon before an unsuccessful attack on Waller's forces at Andover. Royalist troops were left in the city and this led to the only actual fighting in Salisbury in December 1644 and the following January. The King's men barricaded themselves inside the Close but were attacked by Ludlow's men under Major Wansey. Ludlow's memoirs record that the Close gates were set on fire, the Royalist horses seized and

many prisoners taken. In January, Ludlow himself arrived and proceeded to fortify the 220 ft. bell tower in the Close. The Parliamentary triumph was short-lived and the ensuing 'Battle of Salisbury' was little more than a skirmish: Royalist troops arrived at night from Amesbury and surprised Ludlow who returned to the Close for reinforcements to find his own men either in bed or 'taking advantage of the night had stolen away'. With only 30 horsemen, Ludlow entered the Market Place through the narrow passage

66 *Longford Castle was a Royalist stronghold two and a half miles south of the city.*

67 *The Parliamentarians under Ludlow fortified the bell tower in the Close in January 1645.*

behind the Poultry Cross. In the dark, and seemingly under fierce attack, the Royalists fled in terror. Some escaped through the Winchester Street gate, others were trapped in Endless Street, then a cul-de-sac. Eventually, superior numbers counted and the Royalists drove Ludlow's men back to the Close, Ludlow himself escaping over Harnham Bridge. Fighting ended when the Royalists forced a collier to drive his cart of smoking charcoal to the bell tower, which burnt down the door and smoked out the defenders.

Salisbury was occupied for a further five weeks by the Royalists whose behaviour included 'such horrid outrages and barbarities' that they offended 'friends and foes alike'. Many tradesmen lost their entire stock and tools. The troops left in mid-March and, although the city residents still faced sporadic attacks, the fighting was essentially over. Nationally, the turning point came with the Battle of Naseby on 14 June 1645 when the New Model Army proved its technological superiority. By October, Cromwell himself was in Salisbury and the small garrison still at Longford Castle was forced to surrender.

Religious strife lay at the heart of England's civil war and the prelude to the conflict considerably

THE ENGLISH IRISH SOVLDIER

With his new Discipline, new Armes, Old Stomacke, and new taken pillage: who had rather Eate than Fight. 30

IF any Souldate
  think I do appeare,
In this strange Armes
  and posture, as a jeere,
Let him advance up to me
  he shall see,
Ile stop his mouth,
  and we wil both agree.

Our Skirmish ended,
  our Enemies fled or slain
Pillage wee cry then,
  for the Souldiers gaine,
And this compleat Artillery
  I have got,
The best of Souldiers,
  I think, hateth not.

My Martiall Armes
  dealt I amongst my foes,
With this I charged stand
  'gainst hungers blowes;
This is Munition
  if a Souldier lacke,
He fights like *Iohn a dreams*,
  or Lents thin *Iacke*.

All safe and cleare,
  my true Arms rest a while,
And welcome pillage,
  you have foes to foile;
This Pot, my Helmet,
  must not be forsaken,
For loe I seiz'd it
  full of Hens and Bacon.

Rebels for Rebels drest it,
  but our hot rost,
Made them to flye,
  and now they kisse the post
And better that to kisse,
  then stay for Pullits,
And have their bellies
  cram'd with leaden bullets.

This fowle my Feather is,
  who wins most fame,
To weare a pretty Duck,
  he need not shame :
This Spit my well charg'd
  Musket, with a Goose,
Now cryes come eate me,
  let your stomacks loose.

This Dripping pan's my
  target, and this Hartichoke
My Basket-hilted blade,
  can make 'em smoake,
And make them flash & cut,
  who most Home puts,
Ile most my fury
  sheath into his guts.

This Forke my Rest is,
  and my Bandaleers
Canary Bottles,
  that can quell base feares,
And make us quaffe downe
  danger, if this not doe,
What is it then? can raise
  a spirit into fearfull men.

This Match are linkes
  to light down to my belly
Wherin are darksom chinks
  as I may tell yee,
Or Sassages, or Puddings,
  choose you which,
An excellent Needle,
  Hungers wounds to stitch.

These my Supporters,
  garter'd with black pots,
Can steele the nose,
  & purg the brain of plots;
These tosts my shooestrings,
  steept in this strong fog,
Is abl of themselves
  to foxe a Dog.

These Armes being vanisht,
  once againe appeare
A true and faithful Souldier
  As you were ;
But if this wants,
  and that we have no biting
In our best Armours
  we make sorry fighting.

FINIS.

Printed at *London* for *R. Wood*,
and *A. Coe*. 1642.

68 *Citizens suffered from the presence of soldiers. Damage was considerable and houses were plundered. Thomas Lawes lost 'linen and other things to the value of £50', wine valued at £20 and a box of silver plate.*

predates 1642. The struggle between King and Parliament was reflected in religious difficulties in the city. Like other cloth towns, Salisbury was a largely Puritan city in the early 17th century, so the appointment of Archbishop Laud in 1628 with his Catholic leanings caused resentment. Significantly, when John Ivie established the city brewery, the Anglicans in the Close refused to contribute either to the brewery or to Ivie's poor relief experiment. Activities on Sundays, other than attendance at church, were penalised, although the chance of profit sometimes outweighed the threat of punishment: George Tennum of St Martin's suffered 'his wife to sew upon the Sabbath Day and … his daughter … to knit'. The races, despite Puritan condemnation, continued.

The influence of the Church affected the life of the city in a way quite unimaginable today. An incident which achieved national prominence occurred in St Edmund's church. In 1567, Bishop Jewel had ordered that 'idolatrous' stained glass should be removed. For some unexplained reason, the stained glass remained in St Edmund's and, in January 1629, the vestry gave Henry Sherfield, Recorder of Salisbury, permission to take down the window 'wherein God is painted in many places as if he were there creating the world' and to substitute a plain glass window. Despite opposition from the bishop, Sherfield smashed the window with his pikestaff, and in so doing he fell four feet into the pew and was confined to bed for a month. Summoned before the Star Chamber in London in 1633 and accused of disobedience to the Church, Sherfield defended himself saying the window did not truly represent the Creation, showing God 'as a little old man in a long blue coat'. Moreover, he argued, the days of the Creation were out of order. Therefore the window was ungodly and its destruction was lawful. Although evidence was given of Sherfield's good work for the poor of Salisbury, he was fined £500 which was never paid as he died a year later. St

Edmund's church, the stronghold of the Puritan group in Salisbury, was reprimanded for its contempt for the authority of the established church. In contrast, St Thomas's was under the control of the Dean and Chapter. The churchwardens' accounts reveal the differences in their affiliations. Both rang their bells for Charles I's birthday in 1641, but in 1648 only St Edmund's rang for Cromwell's victory over the Scots. With the Restoration of the Monarchy in 1660, St Thomas's paid 18s. for 'ringing on the day the King was proclaimed' and 2s. 6d. for 'washinge the Kinge's armes and making them cleare'.

The fabric of St Edmund's had been causing concern for several years. In 1651, the bell was removed from the top of the tower because it was 'hurtfull to the tower'. Two years later, on 19 June 1653, the danger was considered to be so excessive that 'no peale [of bells] bee rung again'. A week later, the church was full for the morning service with the mayor and 'a great multitude of Godly Christians' in attendance. The churchwardens vividly described what happened: 'The maine pillars did bulge out, and sensibley shake; the cleftes in the walls were seen to open and shutt with Ringing the Sermon Bell that day … so that nothing but the very will of God did keep the Stones and Timver from falling untill the next morning that his one people were all Secure at home, and then hee so sweetly ordered the fall of the Tower that … neither Man, Woman, nor Child, received any hurt thereby'. It was resolved that the 'East end of the Church now standing shall be repaired' while the west end (the former nave), which was damaged beyond repair, should be taken down.

Under the Commonwealth, Salisbury continued to face difficulties and uncertainty. For many, the execution of the King and the declaration of a Republic created a world turned upside down. The Close, given its Royalist leanings, suffered considerably. During the late 1640s acts were passed abolishing first the bishops and then the deans and chapters

69 *The most dramatic event recorded in the churchwardens' accounts was in 1653 when St Edmund's central tower collapsed. By 1656 sufficient money had been raised to rebuild the tower, a rare example of reconstruction in a medieval style under the Commonwealth.*

70 *In 1648 the Bishop's Palace, now the Cathedral School, was sold to William and Joseph Baxter for £88 2s. The building was divided into small tenements, one section being converted into an inn, and the great hall destroyed.*

and their property was confiscated. The Close buildings escaped extensive damage but the Bishop's Palace suffered considerable alteration. Changes in tradition clearly worried many Salisbury citizens. A law of 1653 stated that marriages were to be conducted by a county J.P. or the mayor, with a simple affirmation from husband and wife, the ceremony to follow the publishing of the banns three times, either in a church or in the Market Place. Parish records show that couples preferred the former. Between July 1653 and December 1656 at St Thomas's, only two publications out of 50 occurred in the Market Place, and after 1660 an entry states that marriages 'were celebrated in the old way' and couples no longer had to have their babies secretly baptised.

71 *Portrait of Colonel John Penruddock, Mompesson House. Colonel Penruddock led the disastrous 1655 rising against the Commonwealth. Thomas Mompesson mustered 100 men to support the revolt. While the leaders were hanged, Mompesson was fortunate in escaping and returned to his home in the Close at the Restoration in 1660.*

The uncertainty of the times was reflected in other ways. In 1653, Ann Bodenham, 80 years old, poor, eccentric and 'adicted to popery' was executed at Fisherton Gaol for witchcraft. Five spirits in the shape of ragged boys and the apparent ability to transform herself into a cat sealed her fate as an unfortunate victim of mid-17th-century superstition.

A minority of Wiltshire men were willing to challenge the legality of the Protectorate set up by Cromwell in 1653. A Royalist insurrection led by Colonel Penruddock of Compton Chamberlayne entered Salisbury in March 1655 but received little support from the citizens. The rising collapsed and Penruddock was executed at Exeter for high treason. Of the 'Salisbury rebels', seven were hanged in the Market Place and many others were transported to Barbados and sold to 'inhuman and barbarous persons for 1550 pounds of sugar each'.

The Restoration of the Monarchy in 1660, following the return of Charles II from France, brought further changes. The citizens expressed their loyalty to the king and the royal arms were set up again over the north gate of the Close. Land was returned to the Church, and the bishop and cathedral life were restored. Later in the 1660s, Bishop Seth Ward commissioned his friend, Christopher Wren, to write a report on the fabric of the cathedral. He admired its 'stately and rich planeness' but was concerned about the inclination of the spire and its inherent instability. Another acquaintance of Seth Ward's to visit the city was Samuel Pepys, who admired the 'minster' and the Close. Staying in *The George Inn*, he lay in a silk bed and had 'a very good diet' but found the bill exorbitant including 7s. 6d. for bread and beer. 'I was mad' he wrote 'and came away in that humour'.

The city was still faced with poverty and trade depression. John Ivie, a city councillor for over fifty years, frail and with fading eyesight, was saddened by the failure of his preventative measures. With the

72 *At the Restoration of the Monarchy in 1660, the Royal Arms were put back above the High Street Gate.*

73 *Christopher Wren's notebook, preserved in the Cathedral library, contains this sketch showing the method by which metal bands should be joined.*

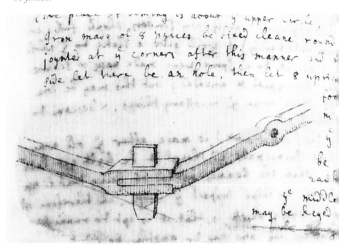

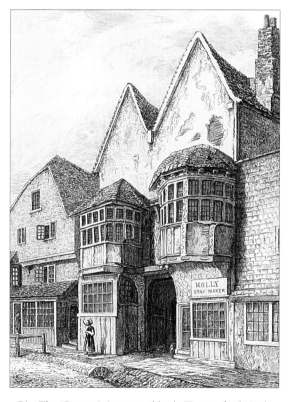

74 *The 'Georgesin' was owned by the Teynterer family in the 14th century. The most important of Salisbury's medieval inns, it belonged to the Corporation from 1413 until 1858. In 1967, the lower storey was partly demolished and the existing carriage throughway widened to allow pedestrian access to the Old George Mall.*

Restoration, Ivie's Puritan principles and work for the poor were pushed to one side. His *Declaration* of 1661 was an attempt to justify his actions and clear his name of unwarranted attacks. Crane Street workhouse continued and in the 1690s Seth Ward gave the Corporation a legacy of £200 'as an abiding stock for the workhouse, to set the poor to work'. New almshouses were built but at the time probably did little more than touch the periphery of the problem.

The religious controversies were not yet over. The Protestant succession appeared secure and a new

75 *Anthony Line was a clothworker in Salisbury. This inventory of his possessions made in 1685 lists, in the back chamber, a feather bed, two feather pillows, a flock bolster, a pair of blankets and a rug, six pairs of sheets, a dozen napkins and a tablecloth.*

76 *The College of Matrons was founded by Seth Ward in 1682 for the widows of 12 clergymen from the dioceses of Salisbury and Exeter.*

R G HEAPE.

Charter on James II's accession in 1685 and expressions of loyalty from the citizens did not indicate the troubled times ahead. There was little support in Salisbury for the Duke of Monmouth's rebellion. However, the unexpected birth of a son to James' Catholic wife meant that the Popish 'threat' loomed again and William of Orange was invited by Parliament to ensure the future of Protestantism. For a short while, in 1688, Salisbury was the centre of the struggle when James established his headquarters at the Bishop's Palace while William proceeded east from Torbay. James's officers, including Lord Churchill, later Duke of Marlborough, deserted him

77 *Blechynden's Almshouses. Margaret Blechynden left money to build a house for six poor widows.*

78 *Alderman Thomas Taylor left £1,000 for an almshouse for six poor single men.*

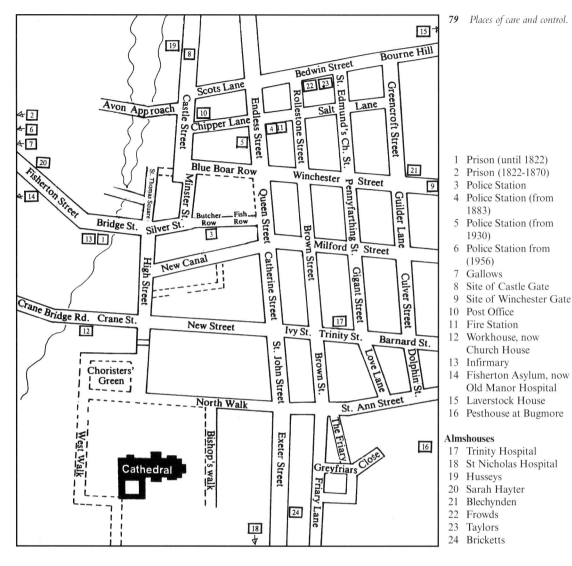

79 *Places of care and control.*

1 Prison (until 1822)
2 Prison (1822-1870)
3 Police Station
4 Police Station (from 1883)
5 Police Station (from 1930)
6 Police Station from (1956)
7 Gallows
8 Site of Castle Gate
9 Site of Winchester Gate
10 Post Office
11 Fire Station
12 Workhouse, now Church House
13 Infirmary
14 Fisherton Asylum, now Old Manor Hospital
15 Laverstock House
16 Pesthouse at Bugmore

Almshouses
17 Trinity Hospital
18 St Nicholas Hospital
19 Husseys
20 Sarah Hayter
21 Blechynden
22 Frowds
23 Taylors
24 Bricketts

and the shock appears to have brought on a severe nose bleed which lasted, according to John Aubrey, 'for near two days' and so impeded his progress. After three days he left for Windsor and William entered the city less than two weeks later to a tumultuous welcome.

VI

An Elegant Society

SALISBURY in the early 18th century was described by Defoe as a large and pleasant city, 'the people are gay and rich, and have a flourishing trade; and there is a great deal of good manners and good company among them'. It was 'full of a great variety of manufactures', alongside the market and other services for the region. Ordinary citizens, as tradesmen, innkeepers or servants, benefited from the growth of a leisured, cultured class of residents and from greater numbers of visitors and tourists. Improved communications contributed to and responded to these developments.

Salisbury was one of the first provincial towns to have its own newspaper. The *Salisbury Postman* appeared briefly in 1715, followed by the *Salisbury Journal* in 1729, published by William Collins, the founder of a dynasty of journal publishers and printers. After an erratic few years, offices were established in New Canal, where they remained until 1962.

By the 1780s, the *Salisbury and Winchester Journal* was well established with a circulation of over 4,000. It originally consisted of four small, closely printed pages and could be consulted at most of London's coffee houses. Two-thirds of the paper was concerned with national and international news with sound editorial 'leaders', while local news and announcements portrayed many of the concerns and issues of the time. Advertisements on the back page often took the form of letters of recommendation for Jackson's tincture for rheumatism or 'easy and

80 A late 18th-century trade token. J. and J. Sharpe, grocers, 'sold fine teas' in 1796. Retailers produced their own tokens when there was a shortage of small denomination coinage.

81 Printing a local newspaper, from Life in an English Cathedral City, *1945.*

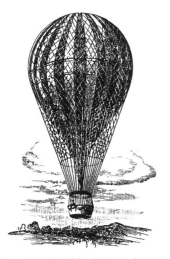

82　*A Grand Aerostatic Globe, the* Journal, *August 1784. A pilotless Montgolfier balloon was launched at the Punch Bowl, Milford. To 'the satisfaction of spectators the balloon continued visible nearly 8 minutes'. It was found 8 miles away and taken to Winchester 'where a live cat was affixed to the balloon … showing the animal as having made the aerial voyage'.*

83　*Barnard's Cross House was advertised in the* Journal, *10 January 1780. 'To be sold, an exceeding good DWELLING house, with good garden, coach house for 2 carriages, … and large wine vaults with good cooperage for carrying on the wine trade – situate on Pain's Hill, lately in the possession of John Thorpe Esq. wine merchant deceased. The vaults are at all times free from water.'*

light wigs for gentlemen and others'. Theatrical news and concerts were regular features as were details of the local Whig landowning family, the Radnors of Longford Castle. Announcements of inoculation and dispensaries for the infant poor jostled for space with 'wanted to purchase – two live bustards' and an unusual venture concerning an air balloon. As with all local papers, crime loomed large and reports ranged from an innkeeper suffering 'tippling in his house during the time of divine service' (fined 10s.) to incidents involving footpads and highwaymen. It is unusual to find advertisements for houses for sale in the 18th century *Journal*, but occasionally one appears, although identification is normally difficult. Barnard's Cross House, with its barrel vaults, on the corner of Payne's Hill, is probably one such building described in the newspaper.

Musical life in the city blossomed during the 18th century largely due to enthusiastic individuals, though music had always played a significant role in the Cathedral. John Aubrey wrote, 'The Quire of Salisbury Cathedral hath produced as many able musicians if not more than any Quire in this nation'. The structured life of the choristers, lay vicars, and organist meant a peaceful environment for creative people, and some exquisite music was made here, though not every creative person was peaceful. Amongst the earlier organists who achieved a national reputation were the two John Farrants, father and son. The elder departed following a knife attack on the dean, his father-in-law, when the latter attempted to intervene in a domestic dispute. In the 17th century Michael Wise was renowned for his hasty temper and inappropriate behaviour: 'Wise doth lye and labour under a notorious Fame of Prophanenesse, Intemperate Drinking, and other Excesses in his Life and Conversacon to ye Great Scandall of Religion and ye Government of this Church.'

Music was also performed outside the Close walls. George Herbert attended a musical group in the 1630s, and by 1700 the Society of Lovers of

Musick was celebrating St Cecilia's Day, a practice which continued into the 19th century. A leading figure was James Harris, who was a great admirer of George Frederick Handel. He ensured that Handel's works featured prominently in the growing number of concerts in Salisbury. Public subscription concerts, and invited audiences in private houses added to the popularity of music as entertainment. Harris developed what has been described as 'the finest society outside London' and attracted among the long list of contributors J.C. Bach in 1773. The regular players included amateur gentry, local professionals, as well as others who travelled from London, Bath and Oxford to play. The army provided both quality musicians, who played woodwind and brass to go with the local gentry's string and keyboard players, and dancing partners at Assembly balls. The king's brother, the Duke of York, visited Harris in 1762, at two hours notice during which they set out 'a very decent supper of nineteen dishes and a very showy desert after'. The Duke was a skilled violinist; after the meal there was 'a little musick which he seemed highly pleased with and played the whole time himself'.

84 *Portrait of James Harris, Gerald Coke collection. James Harris (1709-80) inherited a sufficient income to allow him to devote his time to musical, literary and philosophical interests, and to become an M.P. His eldest son became the first Earl of Malmesbury and the family lived in the Close in what is now known as Malmesbury House.*

Mr Harriss House in the Close of Salisbury

85 *Sketch of the Harris house in the Close from Gertrude Robinson's day book by kind permission of the Earl of Malmesbury. Harris wrote in 1740, 'When Handel was here, I gave him a concert in my house, which was divided into two acts, and consisted of both vocal and instrumental. He did us the honour to give us much applause … Between the acts I got him to sit down at the harpsichord, where he played for near half an hour…'.*

John Marsh was another multi-talented musician who lived in Salisbury between 1776 and 1783. He played with Harris, was a prolific composer and arranger, organised musical events in the city, and took part in another popular form of activity, the Catch and Glee Club. He described the regular weekly meetings at *The Spread Eagle Inn* in the New Canal in 1776: 'there was always a Concert from about half past six till after eight at w'ch time a large Table was set out with Loaves … Cheese and Porter, after partaking of w'ch in rather a rough way, the Company formed a Circle around the fire and Catches and Glees were performed'. Benjamin Banks (1727-95) also contributed to the musical life of the city at this time. He was an instrument maker, principally of violins, but also English guitars, violas and 'cellos, and kits – dancing masters' fiddles. His shop in Catherine Street also sold keyboards and sheet music, and he visited the homes of his customers to tune their instruments, receiving, for example, 10s. 6d. after a visit to Longford Castle to attend to the harpsichord. Banks sold his work through London shops, and received orders for instruments from around the country. The business recovered from a serious fire in 1784 and was taken over by his two sons.

Concerts were only part of the 'genteel amusements' available to citizens and visitors at this time. Assemblies, dances and both amateur and professional drama were popular. Theatres and assembly rooms were attached to inns in the early part of the century. The New Theatre, in New Street, opened with Sheridan's *The Rivals* in 1777. The typical programme at the theatre was a play followed by a farce, with an interval song, entry being half price for the farce only. Comments could be scathing: 'the actors are not quite equal to Mr Garrick', though on another occasion a critic wrote more kindly 'Mr Powell spoke the Ghost [in Hamlet] with great propriety'. Going to the theatre could mean Shakespeare, popular drama, a modern play or entertainments such as

86 *Joan Schmeising (right) and Gemma Russell with Banks' instruments – 1787 violin and 1775 viola respectively. Banks is still held in high regard as an English violin maker. His provincial isolation from others in his field led to the development of a distinctive individual style which made an important contribution to his craft. These two musicians, who are members of the de Vaux Quartet, have the instruments on loan.*

Signora Ricardoni who could stand on her head on the point of a spear! Members of Salisbury's increasingly wealthy and leisured urban élite met at coffee houses such as The Parade in Blue Boar Row; they played cards at social clubs and could patronise the lending library or the Literary and Debating Society for more cerebral pursuits.

Scientfic knowledge evolved at different rates in different disciplines. Bishop Seth Ward, a founder member of the Royal Society, brought with him to Salisbury a reputation in astronomy and mathematics, as well as friendships with Sir Christopher Wren, Sir Isaac Newton and Samuel Pepys. His advanced ideas on elliptical planetary orbits contrasted with his dependence on medical quackery. A contemporary of Ward was Dr. Turberville, who lived in the Close and attracted many who bought his cures for eye disease. Turberville's methods involved a curious mix

87 *An assembly – tea, supper and dancing – was held fortnightly, and a new Assembly Room was opened in 1802 on the corner of High Street and New Canal – above W.H. Smith's (now Waterstone's). Dances were also held in the evenings of special occasions like the races or when the assizes were sitting.*

Many of Salisbury's influential citizens lived in majestic houses in the Close in the 18th century but there were two other residences of particular grandeur: The College, which was built on the site of the 13th-century College of St Edmund's, and The Hall in New Street.

88 *The College (the council house, Bourne Hill) was the largest private house in the city, with its extensive grounds and 'luxuriant and handsome trees', and resembled a country mansion. Owned by the Wyndham family from 1660 to 1871, it was a very desirable residence and was altered considerably in the 18th century to provide the fine Georgian façade.*

89 *Built on the site of the old Assembly Hall, and today rather overwhelmed by modern development, The Hall was built for Alderman William Hussey, M.P. for the city for 39 years. He was benefactor of the Great Room in the Guildhall and founder, in 1794, of Hussey's almshouses in Castle Street.*

Other streets also became fashionable, notably St Ann's
Street. Here, timber-framed buildings were gentrified and
cased in mathematical tiles to simulate brick, and fine new
Georgian houses were constructed. Salisbury was no longer
a growth town, so many medieval structures were left
untouched.

90 Vale House, No. 44 St Ann's Street. A fine symmetrical
town house of five bays built in the late 18th century.

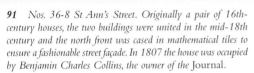

91 Nos. 36-8 St Ann's Street. Originally a pair of 16th-
century houses, the two buildings were united in the mid-18th
century and the north front was cased in mathematical tiles to
ensure a fashionable street façade. In 1807 the house was occupied
by Benjamin Charles Collins, the owner of the Journal.

92 No. 18 St Ann's Street is one of Salisbury's oldest domestic
buildings, being of 14th-century origin. In 1416 it was described as
'an angle tenement with shops opposite the friars' manor'. The house
has original timber framework with 'St Andrew's Cross' bracing, the
only example in the city.

of surgery and fantasy, but his reputation 'brought multitudes to him from all parts of this and the neighbouring kingdoms and even from America'. That was, of course, also beneficial to the lodging houses of the town which accommodated the patients 'wearing green silk upon their faces' making for the doctor's house. At the base of his monument in the Cathedral is the following rhyme:

> Alas! Alas! He's gone forever
> And left behind him none so clever.
> Beneath this stone extinct he lies
> The only doctor for the eyes.

A few decades later, Salisbury was a centre for pioneering work in inoculation against smallpox. The disease was endemic and flared at intervals to cause widespread mortality. Three local doctors were involved in early inoculation, particularly William Goldwyre. Amongst his patients were the Fielding, Craddock and two Harris families, and their servants. It was some time, however, before inoculation against smallpox became universally accepted; in 1752 the medical profession in Salisbury was asked not to inoculate as the inoculees could be a source of infection. But many still believed in its efficacy; Mr. Brown FRS, wrote in 1753, 'inoculation has been much practised here and with great success'. Ten years later a subscription list was opened for a smallpox hospital which was established at Bugmore under the patronage of Lord Folkestone, later the first Earl of Radnor. Eventually at the end of the 18th century, Edward Jenner discovered that the cowpox virus could be used to provide safe immunisation.

The general health of the citizens, particularly the poorer members of the community and the surrounding area, was also a matter of concern. Lord Folkestone's father-in-law, Lord Feversham, died in 1753 and left in his will £500 'to the first Infirmary that should be established in the County of Wilts'. A meeting of benefactors and subscribers was held in 1766, supported by the corporation, the bishop and local dignitaries. Under the chairmanship of the Earl of Radnor it was formally resolved 'that a Society be instituted and distinguished by the name of the Governors of the General Infirmary of Salisbury for the Relief of the Sick and Lame Poor …'. This group acted quickly; houses and land were purchased in Fisherton Street, a matron and two nurses appointed and the first patients admitted by May 1767. Rules for the administration of the hospital were drawn up; the porter, for example, was paid £6 a year and, among his other duties, attended the gate and brewed the beer. Outpatients were forbidden to loiter outside the hospital, and if they came from more than seven miles distance were given 1s. a week towards lodgings in the city to prevent the need to beg. The intentions of the founders were made clear in the choice of motto: 'the sick and needy shall not always be forgotten'. Plans for a new building were accepted from Bath architect John Wood; bricks and tiles were ordered by the thousand and, despite early difficulties, construction continued apace until the elegant new infirmary was opened in August 1771.

In its first year the new hospital treated 192 in-patients and 534 out-patients. They were only admitted or discharged on Saturday mornings and, unless emergencies, came on the recommendation of a governor or subscriber. Many conditions were forbidden – 'women big with child', infectious diseases, and 'all such as are manifestly dying or incurable'. Leeches and hot and cold baths featured prominently amongst the procedures prescribed. For many of the poorest patients the warm building and sound diet were probably as beneficial as any other treatment they received.

The demands in the country at large led to pressures to improve existing transport and Salisbury shared those aspirations. John Taylor, the 'Water Poet', having rowed his wherry from Christchurch to Salisbury in 1623, enthused John Ivie with the idea of linking Salisbury to the sea by making the river Avon navigable, but the project got no further.

93   *The Infirmary in 1771. The original building, proudly announcing that it was 'supported by voluntary contributions', still stands, though now converted into residential apartments.*

Bishop Seth Ward took up the scheme later in the century and 'digged the first spit near Langford House'. By December 1675, two to three hundred workmen 'had digged up all the shallows from Christchurch to Crane Bridge in Sarum', but initial enthusiasm waned, subscribers failed to invest and the council called off the work. The level of traffic was simply insufficient to guarantee success, and by 1730 this attempt to connect Salisbury to the sea by water was over.

Fifty years later Salisbury again attempted to complete a waterway to the south coast. The 1760s marked the beginning of 'canal mania', and in 1770 a canal between Salisbury and Southampton was proposed which would arguably save the city £3,000 a year in the carriage of coal alone. This proved another ill-fated venture, but in the 1790s, at the peak of national canal construction, the scheme was revived. A plan was mooted to construct a 'navigable canal from Bristol to Southampton by way of

Salisbury'. An advertisement in the *Salisbury Journal* of December 1792 offered shares at 5 guineas and two years later £55,000 had been raised. An Act gave the Southampton and Salisbury Navigation Co. the authority to build a canal between the two cities. By 1803 the canal was built and operational from Kimbridge to Alderbury Common but construction problems and a shortage of cash meant that the company became bankrupt and within a few years Salisbury's second attempted navigation to the sea had collapsed in ignominy with only a few traces of the canal left to indicate an expensive failure.

If attempts to improve Salisbury's water transport failed, the story of the roads was more successful. The increase in traffic meant that the city's roads were often in a deplorable state or, as an early 18th-century surveyor phrased it, in a 'sad nasty pickle'. A petition was presented to Parliament from both the corporation and the inhabitants for a bill to enforce the 'cleansing, repairing and paving of the highways,

99   In about 1788 the original Bishop's Guildhall was dismantled. First mentioned in 1314, it was probably one of the earliest public buildings in the new city.

Pomegranate was replaced, and the mail coach drove on. By the 1830s and '40s the golden age of coaching had lost its gilt. In 1840, four coaches left Salisbury daily for London and three went only as far as Andover Road Station. Six years later the Quicksilver set out for London for the last time, and by 1848 the transformation was complete, Salisbury now joined by rail with Southampton and hence London.

The present Guildhall replaced two buildings in the Market Square, the original early 14th-century Bishop's Guildhall and the adjacent Elizabethan Council House. The latter was built in anticipation of the corporation's independence from the bishop, finally achieved in 1612. It went up in flames on 16 November 1780, following a mayoral banquet. The charters and city records were saved, albeit with some water damage, and taken to local houses for

100   North front view (1796) of the Council House, now known as the Guildhall. This was erected between 1788 and 1794 on the site of the Bishop's Guildhall.

safe keeping. No lives were lost and a calm morning meant that surrounding buildings in Blue Boar Row were not affected.

For a short period the council returned to the medieval council house on the north side of St Thomas's churchyard which had been used for much of the 15th and 16th centuries and has long since disappeared. At the same time, the decision was taken to demolish both the damaged Elizabethan Council House and the old Bishop's Guildhall and to build instead a new town hall combining civic and judicial functions. Deciding on its exact location proved to be a protracted process. The second Earl of Radnor, whose family had represented Salisbury in Parliament for over fifty years, offered to finance the new building on condition that it was built to his plan and in the centre of the Market Place. This put the

council in a very difficult position; members did not want to appear ungrateful but neither did they want the new building in the middle of their spacious Market Place. Bishop Barrington intervened and agreed that his Guildhall should be replaced by a 'secular Guildhall' providing that he, the bishop, should have no responsibility for its upkeep. This was eventually accepted and, despite further delaying tactics from Lord Radnor, the Guildhall was built exactly where the council wished and with Lord Radnor's financial backing. William Hussey, Salisbury's other M.P., donated £1,000 for the furnishings to the Great Room. The foundation stone was laid in 1788 and the completed building granted to the mayor and corporation seven years later.

The century ended with the upheavals of the French Revolution and the wars against France. The Dean and Chapter raised £300 by voluntary contributions for 'the defence of the kingdom'. Times were changing even in the smaller world of Salisbury Close. James Wyatt, architect, arrived to 'restore' the cathedral on the invitation of the bishop and the building was closed for three years from 1789. Wyatt, with his passion for symmetry, light and order, destroyed the Hungerford and Beauchamp chantry chapels, pulled down the medieval stone choir screen, rearranged the monuments in neat rows and destroyed much of the 13th-century stained glass. The overall responsibility for these changes lay with Bishop Barrington who donated £500 towards the cost of Wyatt's work whereas the council gave nothing, pleading 'extreme poverty'. The bell tower was removed, Wyatt believing, perhaps rightly, that it detracted from the Cathedral and its Close. Further radical changes came when the bishop ordered the Close to be drained. An earlier visitor had commented that it was like a 'cow-common, as dirty and as neglected and through the centre stagnates a boggy ditch'. The churchyard was raised and levelled and the graves removed. It is said that an army of labourers worked at night unseen, such was the

101   Bust of James Wyatt, architect, who was invited to restore the Cathedral in 1789.

102   The bell tower, in a ruinous condition, was removed, having already lost its timber spire in 1758. An advertisement in the Salisbury Journal *of March 1790 heralded the end of the structure: 'To be sold … the materials, of a very large building … [applications to be made to the] Clerk of the Works … at the Cathedral.'*

adverse reaction of the city to the desecration of the tombs, but Salisbury was left with a beautiful, uncluttered Close.

The changes, especially to the cathedral, aroused huge national controversy. In fairness to 'Destroyer Wyatt' as he came to be called, his ideas did reflect late 18th-century fashion. He was acclaimed as a genius, and the 'Hallelujah Chorus' and the 'Corona-tion Anthem' were sung at the reopening of the cathedral, with George III present, but Henry Hatcher, writing in 1842, perhaps spoke for many Salisbury citizens when he lamented the effects of the alterations on the fabric and railed against those who interfered with historical monuments that 'are the common property of all ages'.

VII

Progress in Difficult Times

DURING THE 19TH CENTURY England changed from a largely rural country to an urbanised, industrial society with its wealth based on coal and iron. The textbook 'industrial revolution' was a long way from Salisbury, however, and for much of the century the community would have been recognisable to John Halle and his contemporaries; this provincial market city had medieval dwellings alongside fine Georgian houses, and attracted artists like Constable and Turner to paint the cathedral surrounded by tranquil water meadows. But the population grew, the city boundaries expanded with the availability of building land and demand for housing, and the economy diversified. In 1801 Salisbury's population was 7,660; by 1851 it had risen to 9,455 and by a further 80 per cent to over 17,000, in 1901. In the next half century it nearly doubled again.

103 *Railway cottages, Waterloo Road. These were built for railway workers close to Salisbury's first line, which terminated at Milford, behind* The Railway Inn, *Tollgate Road.*

By the mid–18th century, the medieval chequers were filled with buildings, and settlements at Fisherton, Harnham and Milford were attached to the city. The arrival of the railway provided employment opportunities and changed the topography of the city as workers' housing was constructed in Fisherton, Milford and Bemerton. An area of land for speculative building became available in the 1870s when 'a substantial family residence with grounds and park of 44 acres' on the north-east side of the city was put up for sale. The expansion of population put pressure on services; St Mark's Church was consecrated in 1899, the first new parish since the 13th century 'necessitated by the remarkably rapid growth of the district'.

The local woollen textile industry had not benefited from the improvements which had affected West Wiltshire and Yorkshire, though flannel production was still flourishing. Salisbury became a service centre for a widespread agricultural hinterland; professional people, traders and craftsworkers responded to the demands of an increasingly prosperous market. Other towns in the region and beyond were growing more quickly, and at difficult times the local economy suffered, but overall the trend showed a successful adaptation.

Cutlery manufacture had been well-established in Salisbury for several centuries. John Aubrey had written that Salisbury was 'ever famous' for razors, scissors and knives. By the nineteenth century it was a small scale, high quality, specialist trade where 'the Royal family and nobility procure their polished steel work'.

Enterprises which produced inputs for commercial agriculture and those which used agricultural raw materials were also important at this time. Ale needed malted grain, and had been produced since the city's foundation. There were small malthouses and breweries attached to inns throughout the city. Williams Brothers was a substantial malting business in the 19th century, on a site of 3.5 acres to the north of Fisherton Street, the area now known as

104 *W. T. White trade card. Umbrellas, whips, guns, baskets, brushes, pipes and watches were amongst the many useful items being made in Salisbury.*

105 *Goddard trade card. 'Let Bristol for commerce and dirt be renowned, At Salisbury let pen-knives and scissors be ground'.*

106 *Salisbury's Exhibition, October 1852. Visitors saw a display which demonstrated the 'enterprise, taste and skill' of local tradespeople as well as museum entries from the collections of neighbouring gentry. An Electric Telegraph demonstration conveyed messages from room to room. Seven thousand people, including school parties and groups of workers treated by their employers, acknowledged with pride Salisbury's achievements.*

107 *The malthouses photographed in 1963. Malting required continuous attention to the grain by a skilled operator as control of temperature, ventilation and humidity was critical to success, particularly on this scale. The works had its own railway sidings where barley arrived.*

108　Joseph Lovibond and his colorimetry equipment. Joseph died in 1918 and his daughters Charlotte, who had married into another local brewery family, the Fawcetts, and Katherine became directors of 'The Tintometer Ltd'. Charlotte's grandson continues the family connection with the business.

109　Henry Wansey criticised the Crane Street workhouse. In his Thoughts on Poor Houses, he offered a mixture of practical suggestions and economies, decreeing that growing parsnips could save the workhouse £300 a year. Children should be kept separate and given education, and weekly visits and reports should be made.

The Maltings. In the years immediately after the Second World War, Williams also malted wheat for Ovaltine. They continued in operation until the 1960s, and the buildings were demolished in 1970 and redeveloped as a shopping area and riverside gardens. Joseph Lovibond came to Salisbury from Greenwich in 1869 to open a branch of his father's brewery. To maintain the quality of his product, he developed a way of measuring the properties of beer by using coloured glass discs. The idea was gradually used more widely and is now an internationally known system of colorimetry. Horsehair weaving was a specialised textile industry which flourished here in the middle decades of the 19th century. Long hairs from horses' tails on a cotton or linen, or occasionally silk, warp made very hard-wearing furnishing fabrics. Children were employed to feed individual hairs to the weavers.

Women were actively involved in many aspects of life in Victorian Salisbury. Domestic service was, of course, the main source of employment. Large households in the Close had as many as nine female

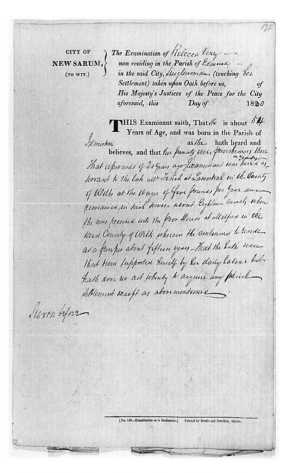

110 *Settlement examination. Paupers had to undergo an interrogation before they were eligible for parish relief.*

servants. Girls as young as 12 worked in smaller establishments too; tradesmen like pipemaker Mr. Morgan employed a house servant. Many independent women were in occupations typical of their gender – milliners and teachers – but there were others in more surprising areas, including manufacturing and construction. Widows commonly took over the family business on the death of their husband, such as Sarah Bedford who had a nursery which specialised in asparagus, and Sarah Rogers at *The Red Lion Hotel*. Those who had leisure time belonged to music and drama societies, they exhibited and won prizes at poultry and flower shows,

and they took part in a great variety of sporting activities.

In the first half of the 19th century, the city experienced religious and political agitation, agricultural riots and cholera. These were troubled years following the long wars against France, when the problems of widespread unemployment, poverty and poor relief became acute. Despite considerable help from the almshouses, the three city parishes provided most of the relief for over 2,000 poor in their own homes and for the residents of Crane St workhouse. In 1801 Henry Wansey described the workhouse as inefficiently managed and overcrowded. The 1834

Poor Law Report endorsed Wansey's findings, describing the workhouse as 'a scene of filth and misrule'. The subsequent Act combined parishes into Unions under elected Boards of Guardians and established 'well regulated' workhouses to act as a deterrent, believing that only the genuinely desperate would apply for relief.

The three city parishes remained as a 'Union' with their workhouse in Crane Street, and a new Alderbury Union workhouse was built in 1836 to accommodate 200 paupers from the Close and 21 other local parishes. Erected on the junction of the Blandford and Odstock roads outside the city, it incorporated many of the strict 'rules' laid down in 1834: segregation of men, women and children, compulsory uniform, and mindless jobs like stone breaking. Local rates fell so the new system was deemed a success.

The city workhouse in Crane Street continued to attract a bad press and was eventually closed. Thomas Rammell's 1851 report described it as 'unsuitable', with an open privy. There was a particular scandal in 1856, when nine-year-old Louisa Garrett died after being placed in a sulphur bath, 'to cure the itch', without medical supervision. The post-mortem concluded that the child had died from 'congestion of the brain' and the case went to the Poor Law Commissioners.

The two Unions amalgamated in 1867. Twelve years later a new enlarged building, known as Salisbury Union Workhouse, was constructed on the Alderbury Union site. Conditions gradually improved and life became more humane, but the stigma remained and fear of the workhouse continued until the system was abolished in 1929. The Crane Street Workhouse had served the city for 242 years but its function changed dramatically when it was purchased by the Church of England, restored by the architect Crickmay and became known as Church House, today the administrative offices of the diocese.

111 Photograph taken in 1956 from the Odstock road, showing, on the left, Meyrick Close Welfare Home, formerly Tower House, part of the Salisbury Union Workhouse. The workhouse, which accommodated 400 people, was constructed at the junction of the Blandford and Odstock roads on the site of the earlier Alderbury Union Workhouse.

The new county gaol was completed in 1822 near the present day St Paul's roundabout. Costing £28,000, it comprised 96 cells and seven courtyards. The old Fisherton Gaol, despite enlargements in the late 18th century, was squalid and overcrowded and the new prison introduced some of the more liberal ideas of the day. Prisoners were classified, cells whitewashed, debtors separated from common criminals, and inspection enforced. Lurid accounts exist of public executions at the gallows nearby but this spectacle was ended in 1855. In the same decade, the stocks in the Market Place disappeared; their last occupant was a drunk, John Selloway, who spent six hours in them on his eighth 'visit'.

112 Radnor House. The gaol continued until 1870 when the Home Office closed it. Part of the building was demolished, but the central block survived as a private residence, Radnor House. It became the Headquarters of Southern Command from 1901 until its demolition in 1959 when the present ring road was planned.

113 The Clock Tower and Infirmary. The ashlar walls at the base of the 1890 Clock Tower were part of the old Fisherton Gaol, built in the 16th century. When the new County Gaol was completed in 1822, the old buildings were purchased by the Infirmary for £1,750 and used as an isolation unit.

ANTI-PAPAL DEMONSTRATION AT SALISBURY.

114   *An anti-Papal demonstration. Despite earlier prejudices, by the middle of the century such opposition was infrequent and Catholics were generally accepted in Salisbury society.*

ANTI-PAPAL DEMONSTRATION AT SALISBURY.

YESTERDAY week (the 22d inst.), the sober, peaceful, and respectable city of Salisbury was frightened from the propriety of its stagnation by a grand mock procession of the Pope, his English Cardinal, and the twelve Bishops, all of whom were afterwards doomed to the flames in one of the biggest bonfires remembered in the West Country. The expenses of this affair were defrayed by a private subscription, and we believe no member of the Church of England professedly took part in the display. The procession was formed at six o'clock in the evening, and commenced its march through the principal streets preceded by a band of music, and attended by a large number of torch-bearers, many of whom were dressed in frocks and cowls, as friars and "monks of old," and wore large comic masks, such as figure in the preliminary scenes of a pantomime.

The effect of this uncouth pageant, as it passed through some of the old streets of the town, lighting up the ancient gables and old wood-work of the houses—some of which date back earlier than the 15th century—was extremely picturesque, particularly when, in its passage along Minster-street, the black and crumbling stonework of the old Poultry Cross came into the picture, looking more black and weather-worn from its contrast with the white illuminated dresses of the Catholic dignitaries, and their torch-bearing attendants.

When the Guys, as the mob irreverently termed these splendid figures, had passed through the greater part of the town, they were carried to a scaffold erected in the Green-croft, the highest open place in the liberties of the city, and there committed to the flames, with fireworks and the usual accompaniments. The populace, who mustered strongly in spite of the rain, which fell at intervals copiously, behaved most decorously. The streets in which dwell the principal Roman Catholics (as also Exeter-street, where stands the beautiful little Catholic church, lately erected from the designs of Pugin) were avoided; and, we believe, no mischief was done, even to the extent of a pane of glass. Let us hope that all who took part in, or were spectators of, this demonstration, did not construe it into *more* than an expression of their loyalty, and their aversion to be priest-ridden; and that they remembered the words of the apostle of the great essence of forbearance — "And now abideth faith, hope, charity, these three; but the greatest of these is CHARITY."—1 Corinthians xiii. 13.

In the 1820s, the 'Catholic problem' – whether Roman Catholics should be allowed to become M.P.s – exercised the minds of the citizens; to many Protestants the nightmare of a Catholic invasion loomed large. As the Catholic Emancipation Bill went through Parliament in 1829, feeling in the city was high. Of the contemporary letters to the *Journal*, 95 per cent were anti-Catholic and the rare ecumenical tract was always attacked. Royal assent was given to the Bill and while many Salisbury Protestants must have awaited their imagined fate, toleration grew. An individual Catholic who appears to have prospered in Salisbury was John Peniston, architect and County Surveyor. An unlikely stalwart of Salisbury society, he wrote of 'becoming really a free man' following emancipation. His religion proved no bar to his success as an architect, nor, more surprisingly, to his position as a commissioned officer

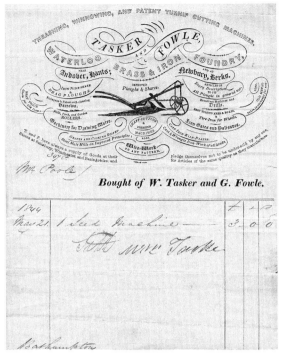

115 *The rioters in 1830 targeted agricultural machinery. In November 1830, Tasker's Waterloo Foundry near Andover was attacked and machinery valued at £2,000 was destroyed. Other rioters sent threatening 'Swing' letters demanding higher wages, or they simply destroyed the threshing machines.*

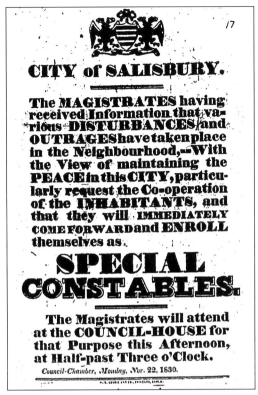

116 *Special constables were signed up from among the 'more respectable members of society'.*

in the Yeomanry cavalry, and he played a leading role in suppressing the 1830 agricultural riots. His acceptance in Protestant Salisbury suggests a man of considerable strength of character.

The year 1830 was extremely troubled as the movement for political change gathered strength. It was, however, the traditionally lethargic agricultural workers who rebelled first as the Swing Riots swept through south and south-east England in the autumn of 1830, with the Salisbury area at the heart of the unrest. Very low wages and little alternative employment meant that many labourers were near to starvation. With a poor harvest and the introduction of the new threshing machines which threatened the labourers' winter work, many became desperate and destroyed the small horse or water-powered machinery. The riots spread rapidly and reached the Salisbury area by 22 November 1830.

Henry Hatcher, writing a few years later, recorded that there was a ring of fires surrounding the city. By 23 November all threshing machines in the neighbourhood had been destroyed. The *Journal* of 29 November carried a front page proclamation by William IV and a separate 'Announcement to Labourers' warning them of their folly, and events were related in full:

> … a party of rioters, after destroying a threshing machine … at Bishop Down's Farm, were proceeding, armed with bludgeons, iron bars and portions of machinery … towards this city, for the purpose … of destroying the iron foundry of Mr. Figes. Mr. Wyndham of the College placed himself at the head of the Special Constables and supported by a detachment of the Salisbury Yeomanry met them at the entrance to the town.

The mob charged but was driven back, the streets were cleared by the Yeomanry and the Guildhall placed under guard all night creating a real sense of crisis. By the end of November, the *Journal* reported, 'We are now, God be thanked, again at peace', but there were 339 prisoners in Fisherton Gaol awaiting trial, mainly for machine breaking. Special Commissions were set up and proceedings for Wiltshire opened at Salisbury Guildhall on 2 January 1831. It was a travesty of justice with John Benett M.P., landowner, acting as magistrate, Chairman of the Jury, and chief witness for the prosecution. The trials were brief and the sentences often severe. Two men at Salisbury were sentenced to death but later reprieved, but 150 Wiltshire men were transported with little hope of return. Whole communities suffered for a generation or more and the repression created long-term feelings of bitterness.

While the agricultural riots were frightening the property owning classes, another struggle was taking place which would have other long-term consequences, the movement for parliamentary reform. The members of the House of Commons in the early 19th century came from a tiny fraction of the population which was out of touch with the people. The rural south was over-represented, while the new industrial cities – Birmingham, Leeds, Manchester – had no M.P.s between them. Old Sarum was simply

118   This reform souvenir was found in the back garden of The Crown and Anchor, *Exeter Street, during the construction of the Friary development. The first Baron Brougham was Lord Chancellor in the 1830 Whig ministry and a leading spokesman on parliamentary reform.*

117   The Parliament Stone, Old Sarum.

a laughing stock, the most rotten of all the rotten boroughs. Seven or fewer voters were granted temporary leases to property (burgage plots) for the day and automatically voted for the owner's two nominees. Already a tourist attraction by the 1780s, an enterprising local family supplied 'the curious who visit with punch, wine and tea'.

Few doubted by 1830 that William Cobbett's 'accursed hill' was an affront to democracy but the battle within Salisbury itself was more complex. The movement to extend the franchise was led by the 'respectable' middle classes, many of whom were denied the vote because only council members had that right. In November 1830, Lord Grey formed a new Whig government committed to reform and for the next 18 months Parliament lurched from crisis to crisis. Reform bills were defeated, governments resigned and at the peak of the crisis, in May 1832, the country appeared to have no government at all. The First Reform Bill was eventually passed in June. It was merely an attempt to disfranchise the worst of the rotten boroughs and to introduce a standard voting qualification which would largely include the middle but safely exclude the working classes. The *Salisbury Journal* was crammed with parliamentary reports as its editor, William Bird Brodie, was a passionate advocate for reform, and became one of Salisbury's M.P.s. The two sitting members were the pro-reform Whig, Captain Pleydell-Bouverie, the Earl of Radnor's brother, and Wadham Wyndham, a

Tory anti-reformer. When the news reached Salisbury that the Reform Bill was to be carried, the editorial made no attempt at neutrality: 'the joy of our townsmen knew no bounds … Salisbury has never in our time known a happier day'. This was followed in June 1832 by a public holiday, and a dinner for 3,000 men in the Market Place. Women, children and the infirm were 'to be provided for' in their own homes.

In the first post-1832 elections, there were 578 electors instead of 58 council members and the constituency was extended to include Milford and Fisherton. The reformers Brodie and Pleydell-Bouverie were returned to Parliament. Though essentially a conservative measure this Act opened the door to further democratic changes.

No.	Christian Name and Surname of each Voter.	Street, Lane, or other Place wherein the Property is situate.			W.	B.	Br.
		ST. EDMUND'S (CONTINUED.)					
78	Everett, Charles William	Endless-street			—		
79	Fulford, John	Castle-street			—		
80	Finch, William	Endless-street			—		
81	Finch, Charles	Winchester-street			—		—
82	Foot, Samuel	Endless-street			—		
83	Fawcett, William	Blue-Boar-Row					—
84	Fitz, Thomas	Blue-Boar-Row			—		
85	Figes, William	Winchester-street			—		
86	Fox, Charles	Milford-street			—		—
87	Foreman, Richard	Milford-street			—		—
88	Griffin, John	Castle-street			—		
89	Griffin, William	Castle-street			—		—
90	Gregory, John	Castle-street			—		—
91	Gillingham, Richard	Milford-street			—		
92	Gillingham, John	Milford-street			—		—
93	Griffin, Thomas	Castle-street			—		—
94	Golborn, William	Blue-Boar-Row			—		—
95	Good, John Everitt	Endless-street			—		
96	Gillingham, Samuel	Milford-street			—		—
97	Hetley, Henry	Endless-street			—		—
98	Hatcher, Henry	Endless-street					—
99	Hill, Stephen	Bedwin-street			—		—
100	Horder, James	Milford-street			—		—
101	Horder, William	Milford-street			—		—
102	Hall, Peter	Winchester-street			—		
103	Hull, Thomas	Church-street			—		
104	Harris, John	Rollestone-street			—		—
105	Hayter, William	Rollestone-street			—		—
106	Hawes, Herbert	Rollestone-street			—		—

119 Extract from The Register of the Persons who voted for Representatives for the City and Borough of Salisbury in December 1832, *being the first election which took place after the passing of the Reform Act. This shows that while Henry Hatcher 'plumped' for anti-reformer Wyndham, the more liberal William Fawcett voted for the two reformers.*

Mid-19th-century political movements were, thereafter, followed closely in Salisbury. In August 1843 leaders of the Anti-Corn Law League, Cobden and Bright, visited the city to attract support, and when Peel repealed the Corn Laws in 1846 there were widespread local celebrations. The mainly working-class Chartist movement formed a Salisbury Association in 1839. There were weekly meetings at the Charter Coffee House in the Market Place with tea or supper parties and debates on such issues as 'Was Jesus a Chartist'? The Salisbury group faded as the movement declined nationally. By this time the *Journal* had abandoned its 'fierce Whiggism' of the 1830s and returned to the position of neutrality followed in the 18th century – 'open to all parties, influenced by none'.

In 1849, Salisbury suffered a cholera epidemic. The city was more densely populated than many large industrial centres with a poor reputation for health. The death rate, at 28 per 1,000, was very high, with property owners worrying about declining house values. Visitors complained increasingly about the state of Salisbury's open water channels, which ran through every street and gave the city the dubious title of 'the Venice of England'. By 1849, these channels had become little more than open sewers. The cause of cholera was still unknown and there was no understanding that it was spread by water. The disease spread like wildfire and 192 people, or one in every 45 inhabitants, died in the epidemic which lasted just under two months. No other town of comparable size in England suffered to the same extent. The *Salisbury Journal* at first denied that cholera was present. When forced to acknowledge the outbreak, it welcomed the fact that the disease was 'thankfully abating' – despite evidence to the contrary. By August 1849, 150 people had died but the paper chose not to mention the fact. Not until attacked in *The Times* (of London) for its censorship did the editor attempt to justify his news blackout. 'We have purposely refrained from comments on a

120   *By 1849 the water channels had become little more than open sewers, and many houses in Minster Street discharged their effluent straight into them. A topographer wrote that 'he'd be inclined to return to Old Sarum to escape the filthy rivulets which disfigure the city'.*

topic painful to … our readers … No one in Salisbury during the past month … can have been indifferent to the progress of the cholera …'.

Panic is said to be 'the parent of sanitation' and cholera had a considerable impact on public health reform in Salisbury. The city's great champion, Dr. Andrew Middleton, battled for improvements. He argued that the evils were wet subsoil, bad water and sewerage. The chequers were filthy, the wells contaminated, and cellars leaked. In 1851, Thomas Rammell, an inspector from the Board of Health, was sent to Salisbury. His report endorsed Middleton's theories and makes lurid reading. The council

APPENDIX II.

Deaths from Cholera, &c. in Salisbury, in 1849; distinguishing the streets in which they occurred. Those marked *o* had open channels, *cl* closed channels, and * no channels.

Castle-street	-	-	*o*	31		
Chipper-lane	-	-	*o*	6		
St. Anne-street	-	*	2			
Gigant-street	-	-	*o*	6		
Rollestone-street	-	*o*	6			
Scott's-lane	-	*partly o*	17			
Milford-street	-	-	*cl*	11		
Catherine-street	-	*cl*	3			
Bedwin-street	-	-	*o*	14		
Salt-lane	-	-	*	3		
Endless-street	-	-	*o*	10		
High-street	-	-	*cl*	5		
The Workhouse	-	*	4			
St. John-street	-	*cl*	1			
Green-Croft-street	-	*	5			
Winchester street	-	*cl*	16			
St. Martin's Church-st.	*	3				

Carried forward 143

Brought forward				143
Queen-street	-	-	*cl*	3
Silver-street	-	-	*cl*	4
Culver-street	-	-	*	3
Brown-street	-	-	*o*	7
Blue Boar-row	-	-	*o*	2
Pain's-hill	-	-	*	1
Oatmeal row	-	-	*	1
Barnard's-street	-	-	*	1
Love-lane	-	-	*	2
Church-st. (St. Edmund)	*o*	11		
Trinity-street	-	-	*o*	2
New-street	-	-	*cl*	2
Penny-farthing-street	-	*	2	
Crane-street	-	-	*	2
Bugmore Hospital	-			2
Ivy-st. (in one house)	-	*	4	
Total	-	-	-	192

Note.—Mr. Middleton supplied me with that part of the above information which distinguishes the streets with open and closed channels respectively, and those with none; the summary under which head appears to be that

114 cases of cholera occurred in streets with open channels.
47 ,, ,, ,, ,, closed channels.
29 ,, ,, ,, ,, no channels.

190

121 (above right) Extract from the 1851 Report on Cholera. Asiatic cholera was a new disease in the 19th century and the most spectacular and dreaded. In less than two months in the summer of 1849, cholera claimed 192 lives in Salisbury.

122 (right) Toone's Court was mentioned in the 1851 Report: 'Mr. Middleton stated that … the channel in Scot's Lane was, for the greater part, open and that the 15 fatal cases of cholera occurred in the houses which were opposite this open part. Out of Scot's Lane is a court called Toone's Buildings, containing six houses, and one double privy, with a pump close to it.'

became the local Board of Health in 1852 and gradually conditions improved. The water channels were drained and filled in, new cemeteries away from the city centre were established in the Devizes Road and at Bishopdown. By 1860, deep sewers were dug, waterworks constructed and houses began to be connected with piped water supplies. The death rate fell dramatically and Middleton rejoiced in helping to destroy Salisbury's reputation as an 'English Venice' since 'many hundreds of human beings [have been] saved from untimely death'.

Until 1899 the city's sewage was discharged into the Avon. A successful action against pollution led to an improved sewerage works at Bugmore which lasted until 1961 when a new system was built at Petersfinger.

The records of the Infirmary follow developments in health care, especially the advances in surgery once antisepsis and anaesthesia were understood. The nursing staff dealt with epidemics and with floods, fleas and rats. From its earliest days the Infirmary provided training for the pupils and apprentices of the physicians and surgeons on the staff, and for nurses. In the 1850s, letters from Florence Nightingale gave advice on nursing and general conditions based on the practice established at St Thomas's Hospital in London, and these improvements were adopted in Salisbury. Through much of its history, the doctors who attended patients at the Infirmary also worked as general practitioners in the city. Other roles included physician to the Workhouse, surgeon to the Salisbury Provident

123 *Salisbury Infirmary. By 1866, the work of the hospital demanded new wings and extensions. Florence Nightingale advised on alterations to both the East and West wings of the Infirmary but there is no record of her ever visiting the hospital.*

124 *'William Finch begs leave to acquaint the public that he has removed to Laverstock House, where he receives … lunatic patients. Laverstock House is delightfully … situated about one mile from Salisbury, opening into a beautiful extensive garden, with every other accommodation for … any lady or gentleman needing such a retreat.'* (Salisbury Journal, 1784)

Dispensary, or Medical Visitor to the Asylum. The next hundred years saw many developments in medicine which led to the establishment of new departments at the Infirmary.

The medical specialism in which Salisbury held a unique position was the care of the mentally ill, and two private asylums meant more psychiatric patients here in the first half of the 19th century than anywhere in the country outside London. Despite conflicting evidence, they seem to have been well run and contradict the stereotypical view of early Victorian asylums. Both were established and run by members of the Finch family. Laverstock House, on the outskirts of Salisbury, which closed in 1955, was purchased in 1779 by William Finch, the founder of the dynasty. Fisherton Asylum – the present Old Manor Hospital – was set up by his son in 1813. The family stressed preventative treatment in a rural environment and 'kindness' was the watchword rather than restraint. In 1842, William Corbin Finch M.D., grandson of the founder, stated that 30 years of non-restraint had produced 'salutary and practical results'. Laverstock House was one of the largest provincial asylums in the country with over 100 patients, both long- and short-term, taking pauper patients until 1851 when the County Asylum

125 *Laverstock House certificate of admission 1834. After 1828, new certificates were required, signed by two doctors, which avoided possible collusion between the family and doctor. Julia Saunders, 'gentlewoman', was 18 when admitted and was removed by her father six weeks later 'cured'.*

at Devizes was built. Fisherton retained its pauper contingent, providing an exceptional diet for them with fresh fruit and vegetables delivered from Bemerton. It also received large numbers of criminal lunatics until 1864 when Broadmoor Hospital was opened. They were paid for by the government and kept in special wards with uniformed male attendants.

Delightful anonymous pamphlets exist for the two asylums. Clearly promotional, they stress personal freedom in a safe and attractive environment, and the apparent happiness of all the inmates. Ironically, both were produced when the institutions were facing criticism. In 1860, a booklet, *Our holiday at Laverstock Park asylum* described the visit of 50 medical men. The patients were compared to 'happy school boys at play', enjoying bowls upon billiard smooth lawns, cricket matches, fly-fishing in the neighbouring streams or outings to the cathedral

and Stonehenge. Both diet and treatment were described in glowing terms; in all a 'model of the very best class of asylums for the insane'. Despite the obvious propaganda, Salisbury's mental health treatment was progressive and the Finch family was at the forefront of such care in the 19th century.

In other ways, too, Salisbury was becoming a safer and healthier place. A gas company was established in 1832 and by the following year Fisherton was enjoying six gas lamps, with other parts of the city following rapidly. Fears of suffocation, poisoning, or explosion were overcome and the Salisbury Gas Company became a safe and prosperous concern. In the 1850s, gas was laid on in Fisherton asylum and gas burners were fitted for the opening of the new Market House. Later, lectures given in the Assembly Rooms on the benefits of cooking with gas were attended by Bishop Wordsworth and his wife. By the end of the century, the Salisbury Electric Light

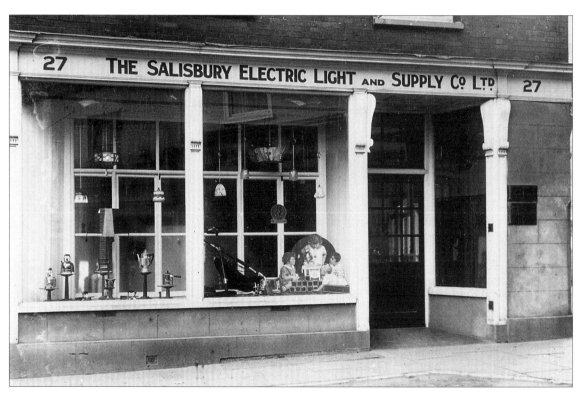

126   Salisbury Electric Light and Supply Company, 27 Market Place, 1929. The shop was in the Market Place from 1923 to 1936.

and Supply Company was generating electricity in the Town Mill, where the sluices and hatches for the turbines can still be seen. A triumphal arch in Fisherton Street announced the advent of free wiring in 1898 and at the complimentary dinner at *The White Hart* 'the tables were illuminated by variegated electric lamps'. Two years later, the Close had electric street lamps.

Nineteenth-century educational provision varied from place to place, and depended both on wealth and on religious affiliation. Classes for the poor often began as Sunday schools. Salisbury's Weslyan Sunday School was catering for 100 children in 1805. Its aim was mainly evangelistic, but attendance gave many children basic skills. Before long, each of the three city parishes had a Church of England Sunday School and by 1833 over 1,200 children were attending across the city. The National Society for Promoting the Education of the Poor in the Principles of the Established Church opened the first voluntary day school in Salisbury in 1811, in a converted malthouse near St Martin's church, and others followed. The children had to come washed and combed, wearing clean clothes, and were expected to bring 1d. every Monday. The origins of education for Roman Catholic children in Salisbury are unclear; 'subscribers to the school' are noted well before the establishment of a school by Lady Herbert in 1867 adjacent to the newly built St Osmund's church in Exeter Street.

From 1833 an annual parliamentary grant was paid to schools through the two voluntary societies, and from the 1860s central government money went to schools on the basis of 'payment by results' calculated by the number of children successfully reaching certain standards. Directories list many 'academies' in Salisbury, some very small, others with many pupils from a wide catchment area. The

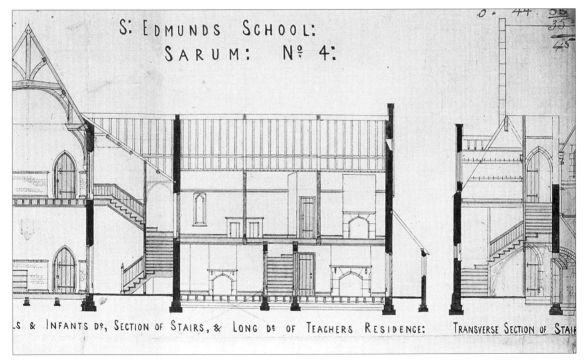

127 *Plan of St Edmund's School. A new school for 500 pupils was built near St Edmund's church in 1860. Boys, girls and infants were taught in separate schoolrooms; adjoining the girls' class was a bonnet room. The school was used for teaching practice by students from the Diocesan Training College, who were provided with a retiring room where they could 'recover their nerves'.*

128 *Portrait of Henry Hatcher, historian and teacher, who described his professional experiences: 'with half-a-hundred noisy and idle youths to superintend it is not possible to give long and steady attention to anything … however there is one comfort; the trade of a schoolmaster is the best point of profit that I have yet exercised and I prefer solid pudding to empty praise'.*

Godolphin School had been founded in 1784, and moved from the Close to Milford Hill in 1847. Henry Hatcher, author of the monumental history of *Old and New Sarum*, opened a school in Fisherton Street in the early 1820s. The Free Grammar School was in serious decline, having only three pupils, in 1864. Working in the recently restored Cathedral with its new organ, the choir school was nationally recognised at the beginning of the 19th century. But in the 1830s the Dean and Chapter reported that '… the education of the Choristers … has been much neglected …'. Fluctuating fortunes continued, but the eventual outcome was a successful preparatory school for both boys and girls.

'Life Long Learning' is a late 20th-century concept but the idea of providing opportunities for education for adults is not new; an appreciation of the economic value of a workforce with basic knowledge and skills came to the fore during the 19th century, and facilities were often sponsored as an act of philanthropy. Several short-lived 'adult-schools' were set up in Salisbury in the early decades of the 19th century. Salisbury Mechanics' Institute held its first lecture in February 1833; scientific apparatus was purchased so that lectures could include demonstrations. Attempts later in the decade to increase the membership by diversifying the programme attracted more middle-class supporters at the expense of the workers for whom it was intended. The Literary and Scientific Institution was founded in 1849, moving in 1871 to purpose-built accommodation in Hamilton Hall in New Street, which later also housed the School of Art. When more new buildings for vocational and technical education were opened in 1895, an exhibition of students' work included woodcarving and plumbing, and the results of an attempt to revive a woollen cloth industry. It was not until 1963 that further education facilities in the city were concentrated on one site when the new Salisbury College of Technology and College of Art buildings were opened on the Southampton Road. Renamed Salisbury College, the programme of courses has developed in many directions.

The Diocesan Training College for female students was opened in the Close in 1841. Amongst the students were Mary and Katherine, two sisters of Thomas Hardy, who based the experience of Sue Brideshead in *Jude the Obscure* on their time there. When admitted in 1860, Mary's 'State of Acquirement' was said to be backward, but she was described as 'diligent', 'improving' and 'persevering' during her time in Salisbury. Both sisters completed the college course and went on to employment as teachers. The trend to larger, mixed higher education institutions with more diverse courses led to the closure of the college in 1978. Many of the buildings were

129   *Training College Students and their bicycles. The Diocesan Training College in the Close, which opened in 1841, supplied female teachers for church schools in the diocese, in parallel with the college for men in Winchester. Salisbury Museum is now located in The King's House, shown above and once part of the Training College.*

converted into pleasant apartments overlooking the cathedral and the river. The Theological College in the Close trained Church of England clergy for 134 years from its opening in 1860 until it too was considered too small to be viable in the modern world. Its successor, Sarum College, maintains the tradition as an ecumenical education and conference centre.

Salisbury was slow to develop railways and early schemes of the 1830s to link Salisbury to Southampton were greeted with little enthusiasm. It took the

completion, in 1841, of Brunel's Great Western Railway (GWR) to generate real interest. The first line to reach Salisbury was the London and South Western Railway's (LSWR) line from Southampton, terminating at Milford. On 30 January 1847, the *Journal* proudly announced that 'a railway train has at length reached this city direct from London'. By March the line was open to passengers and meant huge improvements. The journey to London via Eastleigh now took 4 hours and cost 24s. first class and 18s. 6d. second class. The arrival of the railway

130   *The G.W.R. station saw Salisbury's first railway accident in 1856. The stoker and engineer were killed and there was considerable chaos as the gas lights were extinguished for fear of explosion and attempts to extricate the injured cattle and sheep took place in near darkness. Butchers were summoned to slaughter the injured animals while replenishing their own stocks of fresh meat for sale.*

age was celebrated with a banquet at *The White Hart Hotel* when it was felt that a new era in the city's history was beginning. In an evening of increasingly euphoric speeches it was even suggested that Salisbury could once again regain her former glory as a centre for trade and commerce and 'if they pulled all together' could well become the 'Manchester of the south'. Investors still procrastinated about the construction of further lines.

A broad gauge line from Warminster was completed in 1856, as an extension of the GWR, with a Brunel-designed terminus on the north side of Fisherton Bridge. The line was converted to standard gauge in 1874 and the station finally closed to passenger traffic in 1932. A few months after its opening, the terminus suffered Salisbury's first railway accident involving a heavy cattle train. In the following year, a direct line linking Salisbury to London via Andover was opened so Waterloo could now be reached in 3½ hours. Finally, the Salisbury and Yeovil Railway opened in 1859, 'long delayed and long contested' but an important line which was later extended to Exeter. The Salisbury and Yeovil Company built their station at Fisherton next to the GWR terminus, on the site of the present station. This was then linked with the station at Milford by

131   The London train at Fisherton station in 1945. The Journal *described the station as a 'most commodious building with a glass roof over the platform [which is] nearly 800 feet in length'.*

132   The Market House interior. John Strapp's Corn Exchange, with its glass roof and wrought iron balconies, was a fine building. It was opened on the Queen's birthday, 24 May, when there were appropriate celebrations with the Royal Artillery band in attendance. Special trains were laid on to take guests home after the concert.

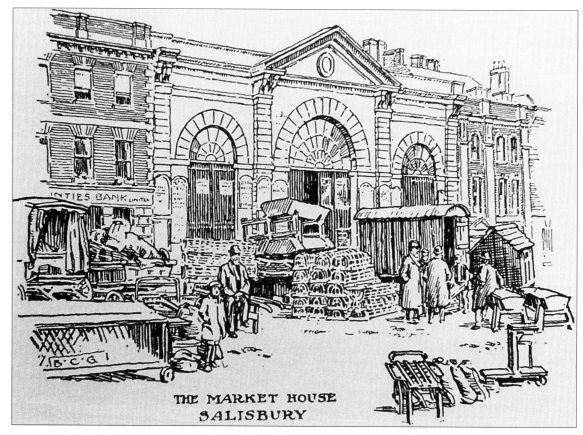

THE MARKET HOUSE
SALISBURY

133   W.H. Hudson in the early 20th century described the Market House as a 'huge beehive' of activity on market day but, despite his observations, its trade was never enormous although it and its railway continued to function until 1964. The façade was preserved as part of Salisbury's new library.

means of a new bridge across Fisherton Street and a tunnel. Milford became a goods station, eventually closing in 1967.

By the late 1850s, Salisbury was the focus of a busy railway network. The market and the business centre of the city were felt to be too far from the stations and in 1859 a short branch line was opened to a splendid covered market house, at the west end of the Market Place, so that corn, cattle and cheese, but never passengers, could be brought into the heart of the city. Salisbury failed to become the 'Manchester of the south' but remains an important junction.

VIII

Adapting to a Modern World

✧

THE CHARTER OF 1612 remained the basis for local government in Salisbury until the Municipal Corporations Act of 1835. This established a council with a mayor, six aldermen and 18 councillors, equally representing the three wards. Councillors were elected by the ratepayers, and the mayor and aldermen chosen by the council. The functions of the new council continued much the same but its jurisdiction covered the parliamentary borough, thus including parts of Fisherton, Milford and the Close. Councillors were responsible for the city's property, the market and fairs, law and order, and the municipal charities. The mayor and aldermen acted as Justices of the Peace and presided at the city's Quarter Sessions which had both judicial and administrative responsibilities.

During the first few months of 1895, as an illustration of their duties, the mayor and corporation attended the opening of the technical education buildings (wearing their new three-cornered cocked hats), discussed how to deal with the distress caused by a period of severe weather, transferred various brewery licences at the City Petty Sessions, and welcomed the bishop back to Salisbury after his world tour. Land was made available for allotments from 1909. The Salisbury Volunteer Fire Brigade was taken over in 1920, and in 1924 Fisherton Anger and Bemerton Water Works came under council control. In 1927, Salisbury had its first female mayor, Lady Hulse, and in the same year the city marked the 700th anniversary of the charter granted by Henry III and the new Council House in Bourne Hill was opened during the celebrations. Changes after the Second World War gave the county responsibility for education, the police and fire services, and welfare functions of the city. Local government reorganisation in 1974 created Salisbury District Council, which has powers over most of south Wiltshire.

Main extensions of
city boundaries

: : : :	City area pre-1835
* * *	boundary 1835
◇ ◇ ◇	boundary 1904
△ △ △	boundary 1927
+ + +	boundary 1954
——	boundary 2000

134 Map showing change in boundaries. The growth of the population was recognised with the extension of the city boundaries. The size of the council increased as more wards were represented.

The 1888 Local Government Act raised the question of which was the premier town of Wiltshire. The first meeting of the new County Council was held in Salisbury, but the subject of a regular meeting place came under animated discussion, including the comment that 'people thought it was a greater distance to go from Salisbury to Swindon than to go from Swindon to Salisbury'! It was not until 1900 that the staff and council were concentrated in Trowbridge.

135 *The new police force was established in 1836 based on Robert Peel's Metropolitan Police. There was to be a superintendent, four day police and 14 night police. The force was to have a blue frock coat and top hat 'with the arms of Salisbury on one side of the collar and the number on the other'.*

As a result of the changes in local government a new police force was established in 1836 with wider powers than the watchmen who had previously patrolled the streets at night. Salisbury was unique in Wiltshire in that its force remained entirely separate from the County Constabulary until 1946. Despite frequent criticisms from government inspectors, including accusations of drunkenness among constables, the force continued to expand. In 1883, a new police station was built in Endless Street where it remained until moving to Wilton Road in 1956.

The Salisbury Municipal Fire Brigade was supplemented from 1884 by the Salisbury Volunteer Fire Brigade, whose members left their many occupations in the city, or their beds, when called to attend a fire. Five years later the two groups were merged, and described as 'one of the most useful institutions in the city' due to their reputation for prompt attendance at many blazes in the area. Their first motor fire engine, acquired in 1913, was named 'Fawcett' after Captain Sidney Fawcett who had been their commanding officer for many years. In 1941 the brigade became part of the National Fire Service, moving to a new station in Ashley Road in 1964.

The second half of the 19th century saw a renewed interest in parliamentary reform. In 1866 William Gladstone visited Salisbury and presented his Reform Bill to a packed meeting staged by local Liberals, but it was his great rival Disraeli who passed a far more radical bill the next year. The borough electorate approximately doubled, and Salisbury was left with two M.P.s, but this was reduced to one by the Reform Act of 1884. The city was dominated by the Liberals from the 1850s to the mid-1880s and then followed a long period of Conservative representation except for the great Liberal heyday of 1906-10. Prime Minister Asquith campaigned in the city in the January 1910 election as Salisbury was an important marginal seat. There was a 97 per cent turnout; the Tory candidate was successful and since then Salisbury has consistently returned Conservative M.P.s. The present incumbent, Robert Key, has reverted to the 19th-century tradition of being 'a local man'.

Women were also involved in politics, and from 1867 unmarried women ratepayers could vote in municipal elections. Although none in Salisbury stood for election before the First World War, they did propose candidates, and were said to present a good turnout at election time. They were also Poor Law Guardians, or active in the Temperance Society or the governing bodies of the Training College and of local schools. Organisations such as the local branch of the Primrose League and the Salisbury Women's Liberal Association gave women a role in national party politics before they had a parliamentary vote.

136 *Advertisement for Scout Motors, December 1909, Salisbury Journal. Even advertisements reflected the excitement of the January 1910 election and both Liberal and Conservative candidates addressed Scout employees. This example carefully avoided political allegiance!*

137 *The Labour Party candidate in the 1950 general election was W.A.J. Case, seen here speaking on the Guildhall steps. Labour first contested the constituency in 1924. Bill Case came second in 1950 to John Morrison, who successfully defended Salisbury for the Conservatives at seven elections.*

TARIFF REFORMERS & FREE TRADERS

are BOTH AGREED in their opinions of

"SCOUT" CARS

namely, that they are equal to any of the highest priced Cars on the market, and at <u>their</u> price they are the best value obtainable for money.

BRITISH MADE THROUGHOUT.   SUPPORT HOME INDUSTRIES.

CATALOGUES POST FREE ON APPLICATION TO

THE MANUFACTURERS:—

"SCOUT" MOTORS, LTD.,

" SCOUT " WORKS, SALISBURY.

TELEPHONE:—No. 48.   TELEGRAMS:—" SCOUT."

The Salisbury Women's Suffrage Society was formed in 1909, shortly followed by the Salisbury and South Wiltshire Branch of the National League for Opposing Women's Suffrage. There were few supporters here of the militant tactics of the Pankhursts, but the enthusiasm in promoting suffrage was no less for being channelled through more constitutional lines. Many meetings were held, addressed by national and local speakers such as Millicent Fawcett and Fanny Street. Women over 30 were given the vote in 1918; that summer a special service was held in the cathedral 'to seek the Blessing of God on the responsibilities resting upon the women of the country … consequent upon their recent enfranchisement'.

Progress for both men and women depended increasingly on educational achievement. The 1870 Education Act provided for the election of local school boards with a duty to guarantee school places for the children in their area and, if necessary, to establish schools to fill the gaps. Salisbury School Board had seven members, typical substantial citizens. It was calculated that there were 2,294 children requiring elementary education and sufficient schools for them. Local by-laws made attendance compulsory in 1872 and this became a preoccupation of the Board. The threat of a visit from the Attendance Officer, however, was no match for the need in many families for children to be at work, for epidemics such as scarlet fever, or for alternative attractions such as Salisbury fair – all reasons for absence given in St Martin's School log book at the end of the century. There never were any board schools in Salisbury. A serious shortage of places arose in 1888 when the British School failed an inspection and had to close. Nonconformist interests pressed for the foundation of a non-denominational board school financed by the rates. Salisbury Church Day School Association was formed, and the bishop, John Wordsworth, led a campaign to maintain Anglican control over the schools, rashly remarking that 'as long as he was

Bishop, he would never allow board schools to be introduced into this town'. The debate reached the pages of *The Times* and the floor of the House of Commons, and was only resolved with the building of three new church schools for elementary pupils and Bishop Wordsworth's School for higher grade students, all opened in 1890.

Under the 1902 Education Act, Salisbury became responsible for its own elementary education. The first new school was built in Highbury Avenue in 1924, and 16 years later Devizes Road Infants and Juniors' School opened to serve an area of fast-growing population. Bishop Wordsworth's School accepted girls, and took advantage of provisions in the 1902 Act to become a Secondary Grammar School. Lack of space caused overcrowding which was eased by Wiltshire County Council opening South Wilts Girls' School at Stratford Road in 1927. Steps towards 'secondary education for all' were taken when St Edmund's and St Thomas's Schools became senior schools for girls and boys aged 11-14 respectively.

There was more reorganisation following the 1944 Education Act and more change as schools were relocated on the outskirts of the city in the following decades. In the second half of the 20th century there were numerous proposals to redevelop secondary education in Salisbury along comprehensive lines, prevented on each occasion by local pride in the two grammar schools. In 1975 the western part of the city was reorganised into a three-tier comprehensive pattern, while elsewhere the 11-plus examination continued to select children for places at Bishop Wordsworth's and South Wilts Grammar Schools. Since then the geographical divide has softened, and the selection examination is open to children at 11 from any city schools. The continuing presence of a varied independent sector adds diversity to educational provision in Salisbury into the 21st century.

The internal appearance of the Cathedral was changed dramatically through the work of Wyatt

138   *Early 19th-century drawing of exterior of St Edmund's
Church Street Methodist church.
John Wesley first visited Salisbury
in 1738, supporting the expanding group of Methodists here,
who built their first church in St
Edmund's Church Street in
1759. Francis Asbury, who
founded the Methodist Church in
the USA, was Superintendent of
the Salisbury Circuit before setting
out for the New World in 1771.*

(and, to a lesser extent, of Gilbert Scott in the 1860s) and services gradually altered too, increasing in number and in the degree of participation of the congregation. Bishop Hamilton preached in the Cathedral nave to the congregation for the first time in 1861. Not until 1915 were evening services held there, though they were a feature of St Thomas's. The Church of England responded to the growth of population in the city by setting up temporary churches in Gigant Street in 1880, and in Winchester Street and the Friary in the 1890s. When the first part of the new church of St Mark's came into use, St Martin's donated a 17th-century pulpit. In the 1930s St Francis's parish was created to meet the needs of another growing neighbourhood. Comments that church buildings were in urgent need of repair led to the formation of a Church Building Association, which provided grants. Conditions certainly needed to improve if 'many who came to worship in the winter brought horse rugs with them to prevent them shivering with cold'!

In 1851 there were three Methodist, two Congregational, a Baptist and a Swedenborgian church as well as five Anglican and one Roman Catholic. Churches drew their support from across the city. Brown Street Baptist church, for example, at the time of a new building in 1829, had amongst their trustees 'businessmen, taking their share in the city's commercial life and bringing to their Church their business acumen'. Mr. Pye-Smith, a Baptist who was mayor in the 1890s, lived at No.11 The Close, suggesting that it had become a socially desirable address rather than a place of residence for cathedral officials. The Brown Street pastor for the last 30 years of the 19th century was described as a 'fighting Liberal' and three clergymen appeared at a meeting to support the formation of a branch of the Church League for Women's Suffrage in 1912.

The very first Salvation Army band was formed in Salisbury in 1878, but Salvationists were not welcomed. Public opinion towards them gradually became more sympathetic. The Salvation Army hall was opened in Salt Lane in 1883 and by 1887 the band was invited to play at the Salisbury celebrations of Queen Victoria's Jubilee. When the practice of Roman Catholicism ceased to be illegal in 1771, services were held by a Jesuit priest in Mrs. Arundell's house in the Close with a congregation of some dozen people. As numbers increased, larger accommodation was required and after several moves,

139   The Salvation Army Band faced problems. In February 1881 the Justices forbade meetings because of opposition from a 'Society for the Suppression of Street Parading' whose tactics included hurling missiles of 'mud and snow, artistically combined'.

a chapel was built off St Martin's Church Street. By the 1840s discussions were underway on a new church. Augustus Pugin took time off from designing the new Houses of Parliament to provide plans, a site was found in Exeter Street and St Osmund's was opened in 1848. Prominent Catholic citizens provided substantial financial support, including John Lambert, a solicitor, who would become the city's first Catholic mayor since the Reformation.

Eighteenth-century bookshops, such as Eastons in Salisbury, often operated as libraries, appreciating

TO THE INHABITANTS OF THE
CITY OF SALISBURY.

FELLOW CITIZENS,

We have endured for a considerable time the noise and nuisance caused and created by the proceedings of THE SALVATION ARMY, through their perambulating the Streets of our City, notwithstanding which we have patiently kept from resorting to any measures of opposition in the earnest hope that the governing body of this City, would in accord with the popular desire. PUT A STOP TO THE NUISANCE thus created; but that patience has been exercised in vain; the governing body of this city have failed to move in the matter, and will not yet put in force the power which they possess FOR THE STOPPING OF THIS NUISANCE!!! We therefore wish it to be known that a Society has been formed for the purpose of doing what the executive fail to do. Their sole object will be

To STOP the Parading of the Streets by the SALVATION ARMY.

They will employ various ways and means with which to accomplish this end. They will cause to be forcibly broken the ranks of the Salvation Army when in Procession through the Streets, and they will use every means in their power TO STOP AND RESIST THOSE PROCESSIONS FROM SO DOING. At the same time they will give such advice and instructions to those whom they may employ, or those whose sympathy and help they enlist, to have due respect for their persons, especially more so those of the weaker sex. But although they will so advise them, they will not be responsible for what may arise, should they be first assaulted. This Society will also assist any one or more (should they become involved in any difficulty through their exertions on their behalf), both pecuniarily and by other means, so as that they be not wrongfully used. This Society will not in any way countenance any difficulty which any one or more may bring to his or themselves INSIDE OF THE SALVATION PLACE OF WORSHIP, which this Society thinks both a FIT AND PROPER PLACE FOR THEM TO KEEP TO. This Society therefore calls upon all those Citizens who are able to assist them in any way so to do, and by combining together and FORCING THE SALVATIONISTS to do what the Executive are so loth to do, TO BRING BACK THAT PEACEABLE & QUIET STATE OF THIS CITY, WHICH PREVIOUS TO THE EXISTENCE OF THIS NUISANCE, WAS

A PATTERN TO THE NATION.

Given under our hands this 18th day of February, 1881.

FREDERICK RODWAY, Chairman
SAMUEL HOWE, Secretary

To the Society for the Suppression of Street Parading.

the additions to profits from hiring as well as selling books. Other businesses – printers, artists, even milliners – loaned books to wealthier customers for a substantial annual subscription. The Salisbury and South Wiltshire Library and Reading Society was founded in 1819, accumulating some 4,000 volumes in the next thirty years. A lending library for 'mechanics, servants and others', established by the S.P.C.K. in 1826, was short-lived, but a 'library of useful books' accessible at low cost in the Mechanics' Institute prospered. The Salisbury Literary and

Scientific Institution provided a library, and, from 1855 to 1871, a programme of lectures and demonstrations at a moderate fee, and introduced successful 'Salisbury Readings'. In 1862, they arranged to put a book collection in the Police Station.

Until 1905, Salisbury Public Library was located in Endless Street, over Webb's furniture store. Inconvenient access and opening hours, and the lack of space, generated pressure for a new building. After lengthy discussion of alternative sites, Chipper Lane was chosen and the new library built. Through the

140 *Laying the foundation stone of the new library in Chipper Lane, 1904. This was made possible by a grant of £4,000 from the Carnegie Trust.*

century, the book collection expanded; a specialist children's department was added, and the library played a central role in the life of the city, as a popular meeting place as well as a vital source of information and pleasure. The redundant Market House was selected for a new library, and a state-of-the-art facility was opened in 1975. Videos and CDs can now be borrowed as well as books, and information is available on paper and on-line.

142   Members of Old Sarum Archers, formed in 1791, dined together after a shoot 'in harmony, festivity and loyalty'. Archery was a widely supported and highly organised activity in the 19th century, and one in which both men and women took part. This photograph shows the Grand Western Archery Championship meeting in Salisbury in 1862.

141   The Salisbury, South Wiltshire and Blackmore Museum. Frank Stevens, Director of the museum, entertains visitors in 1945. In the case is the drainage collection which began the museum – the detritus of everyday life, buckles, spoons, keys, which had fallen into the water channels in the city streets.

One unlikely result of the drainage of the water channels was the founding of the city's first museum. Considering the wealth of archaeological sites in the vicinity, it is perhaps surprising that Salisbury did not have one sooner. In 1859, a few enterprising gentlemen paid £32 10s. at auction for 'the ancient relics' from the city channels. These were first housed briefly in 1 Castle Street, and moved to St Ann's Street in 1864. In 1867 Dr. W. Blackmore's collection was opened in a neighbouring house and before long the two museums were effectively operated as one. Financial difficulties had to be faced at times, and as the collections grew, and as ideas about conservation and display developed, the buildings became desperately congested. After the closure of the Training College, The King's House in the Close became a new home for the Museum in 1981 in a suitably historic setting.

Leisure facilities for the citizens of Salisbury grew apace during the 19th century, the increasing variety reflecting the demands of different sections of society. By the end of the century it was possible to join a

political organisation of any hue and interest groups such as the Salisbury Temperance Association. The churches all had their associated social and educational activities. Some clubs required more energetic involvement – the Rowing and Sailing Club for example – and others less, such as the Philatelic Society. Cycling was an increasingly popular leisure activity from the 1880s. The Salisbury Cycling and Athletic Club was formed in 1885 for the purpose of 'enjoying a ride in the country once a week'. Many lady cyclists in Salisbury came under the care of Mrs. Edwards, who provided cycling lessons to introduce the new machines. Gardening, fly-fishing, pigeon-fancying could all be enjoyed under the auspices of a local organisation, as could golf, cricket, football and rugby. A newly formed Ladies' Cricket Club appeared in 1911 to join the Ladies' Rifle Club and Ladies' Swimming Club.

No doubt people in Salisbury had always swum in the rivers on a hot day, but in 1892 there was at last a purpose-built indoor pool. This was in Rollestone Street, and the water was heated by steam from the laundry next door! During the winter the pool was covered and became the Victoria Hall, which provided a skating rink and a large venue for meetings and entertainments. A swimming area was built by the river behind the Town Mill in the 1920s, and ten years later, further north off Castle Street, was opened the outdoor pool which would dwell in the memories of school children for the next forty years. The new indoor pool opened in 1976 behind the Council House was luxurious in comparison, but it too will be replaced early in the 21st century by a pool complex at the Leisure Centre.

The therapeutic effects of fresh air and exercise were appreciated by the Victorians, and places like Old Sarum were popular walks for Salisbury residents and visitors. In 1892 the monument came under the care of the Office of Works to be preserved for the nation. The Greencroft had effectively been a public open space for centuries, but in 1882 it was formally given to the city. Riverside Walk, later Churchill Gardens, and Queen Elizabeth Gardens all added to the facilities in the 20th century. Harnham Hill with

magnificent views of the city was the site of the accident which blinded the Liberal M.P. Henry Fawcett. Queen Victoria's Golden Jubilee was commemorated by the opening of a recreation ground, Victoria Park. Land was purchased from the Dean and Chapter in 1887, after £2,200 was collected door-to-door. In 1905 it was handed over to the city to be maintained from public funds. When the College of St Edmund's became the property of the corporation in 1927, not only were there new council offices, but also 'a delightful park for the elderly' and 'playing fields for organized games in the heart of the city'.

The Market Place provided the ideal venue for large-scale celebrations. There was a vast bonfire there in 1855 after the fall of Sebastopol. The Coronation

144 Henry and William Fawcett. Despite his disability, Henry Fawcett was Professor of Political Economy at Cambridge and Postmaster General in Gladstone's Liberal Government of 1880. He campaigned for compulsory education, and votes for women. His father William was mayor of Salisbury at the time of the 1832 Reform Act.

145 Victoria Park, 1902. The construction of Victoria Park in 1887 was a true community effort. A bazaar raised money for building facilities like the cycle track; the mayor gave the materials for the bandstand; Sir Edward Hulse donated the south gate; all the trees and shrubs were given by individual benefactors; free labour got the work done.

146 The First Wiltshire Rifle Volunteers fired a feu de joie *in front of the Guildhall to celebrate Queen Victoria's Golden Jubilee in 1887, followed by a procession and public dinner. The tables can be seen set ready beyond the crowd.*

of Edward VII in 1902 was marked with an open-air dinner for men, after a splendid pageant had paraded through the streets. Women and children were given a tea party in Victoria Park where 50lb of tea and a ton of cake were consumed!

Despite the lull in the musical life of the city after the death of James Harris, opportunities to attend concerts were soon again available to Salisbury citizens. A Salisbury Philharmonic Society (1839) and Sarum Choral Society (1848) were formed, and others followed. Concerts were held to celebrate many events and to raise money for worthy causes. In 1895, the restoration of George Herbert's church at Bemerton benefited from concerts at the Assembly Rooms, at which 'Mrs. Helen Trust, … notwithstanding the fact that she was suffering from a severe

cold, had no difficulty in winning prompt recognition of her delightful singing and charming manner'. Salisbury Amateur Operatic Society was formed in 1908 for the purpose of giving annual operatic performances in aid of funds for Salisbury Infirmary. An eclectic mix of classical and popular music continued to entertain the citizens through the 20th century. Famous groups of the 1960s came to swinging Salisbury including the Beatles and the Rolling Stones; by then the City Hall had become a favoured venue, with the Alexandra Rooms in St John's Street providing a more intimate atmosphere.

The New Theatre in New Street continued to present drama to Salisbury audiences until 1863. Touring theatre companies also came to the Assembly Rooms, and from the early 1870s to the Hamilton Hall. In 1889, the County Hall was opened on the corner of Chipper Lane and Endless Street, and it was here that the first films in Salisbury were shown in 1908. It was renamed the Palace Theatre in 1910, and two years later was described as having 'an exceptionally well-appointed stage' and seating for 1,200. Like concerts, plays were used for celebrations and fund raising. The grounds of The Brambles in London Road, now demolished and replaced by flats, saw a performance of *Romeo and Juliet* by the Avon Players in 1913 in aid of St Mark's Church Building Fund.

The silent film industry satisfied longings for escapism during the First World War but the Picture House in Fisherton Street opened with a showing of the official war film on the Somme in 1916 telling of 'superlative heroism, wondrous endurance and glorious sacrifice'. It was the nearest most audiences came to the violence of modern warfare. The inter-war period saw the development of the cinema as one of the most popular forms of entertainment. Competition from large organisations meant that

147 The coronation of Edward VII in the hot summer of 1902 was celebrated with a dinner for men in the Market Place and a tea for women and children in Victoria Park.

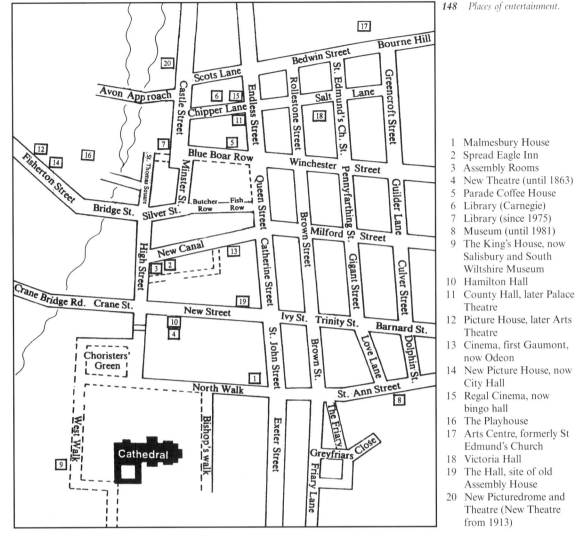

148   Places of entertainment.

1   Malmesbury House
2   Spread Eagle Inn
3   Assembly Rooms
4   New Theatre (until 1863)
5   Parade Coffee House
6   Library (Carnegie)
7   Library (since 1975)
8   Museum (until 1981)
9   The King's House, now
    Salisbury and South
    Wiltshire Museum
10 Hamilton Hall
11 County Hall, later Palace
    Theatre
12 Picture House, later Arts
    Theatre
13 Cinema, first Gaumont,
    now Odeon
14 New Picture House, now
    City Hall
15 Regal Cinema, now
    bingo hall
16 The Playhouse
17 Arts Centre, formerly St
    Edmund's Church
18 Victoria Hall
19 The Hall, site of old
    Assembly House
20 New Picturedrome and
    Theatre (New Theatre
    from 1913)

both the Palace in Endless Street and the New Theatre in Castle Street closed down in the early 1930s.

In 1931, the Gaumont British Wonder Theatre opened in New Canal with *A Yankee at King Arthur's Court* and this cinema, renamed the Odeon in 1962, has survived together with its unique 15th-century foyer. John Halle's views can only be surmised!

Salisbury's two other new cinemas of the 1930s have not been so fortunate. The growth of television meant dwindling audiences from the 1950s. The New Picture House in Fisherton Street showed its

last film in 1961 and became the City Hall, offering a varying range of entertainment from wrestling to opera. The Regal in Endless Street, a vast cinema seating 2,000, became a bingo club in 1969. The Odeon came under threat in the 1970s and '80s but a new lease of life in the late 20th century means that, with five screens and healthy audiences, its future and prosperity in its medieval setting seem assured for the foreseeable future.

No one seemed to want the old building which had been the Picture House in Fisherton Street until it was given a new identity as the Garrison Theatre

149 *A 1930s drawing of the Gaumont Picture Palace, now the Odeon Cinema.*

of Southern Command in 1943. A sparkling array of stars appeared to entertain the troops – including Laurence Olivier and Peter Ustinov. After the war the Salisbury and District Society of Arts reopened the building as the Arts Theatre; it became The Playhouse in 1953 and was replaced in 1976 by the new Playhouse in Malthouse Lane. An entertaining and stimulating repertoire is on offer and traditions such as the support of the theatregoers club and the annual pantomime have become firmly established.

The 13th century Deanery in the Close is now The Medieval Hall, with acoustics of such high quality it is in demand for classical music broadcasts and recordings as well as live concerts and lectures. When St Edmund's church was declared redundant

by the diocese such a significant building for the history of Salisbury could not be allowed to decay, so it found a new role as an Arts Centre, opening in 1975 with a programme ranging from exhibitions, gigs and poetry readings, to the Salisbury Beerex and book fairs. More recently a nonconformist chapel in Milford Street, after many years of neglect, has become a successful nightclub.

Transport became increasingly important to Salisbury's new identity, but in 1906 a railway disaster shocked both city and country, comparable in severity with the 1999 Ladbroke Grove accident. Competition between companies to capture traffic led to continual reductions in journey times and, on 1 July, the LSWR's boat express from Plymouth to Waterloo failed to negotiate the reverse curve coming through Salisbury station. It collided with an oncoming milk train and then struck the girders of the bridge over Fisherton Street. Twenty-eight people died, mainly North Americans, and the

150 *The Arts Theatre became The Playhouse in 1953.*

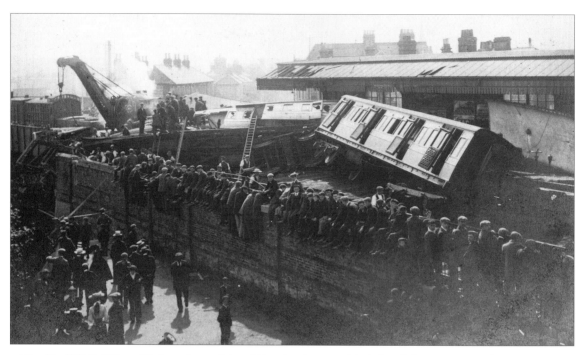

151 The 1906 Rail Disaster. The Journal *reported that within a short time most of the city's medical men were in attendance. Waiting rooms were used as both surgeries and mortuaries and rescue was hampered because of darkness. The tragedy warranted a special supplement with photographs in the* Journal *and is commemorated by a plaque in the cathedral.*

Infirmary received a personal letter of thanks from President Theodore Roosevelt for its treatment of the injured.

Railways effectively destroyed both stage coaches and canals but increased the trade of the humble carriers who have been described as both 'omnibus and shopping agents'. Goods were delivered from railway stations to outlying villages and Kelly's 1889 Directory for Salisbury listed 112 carriers operating 233 services. Those from nearby villages managed the return journey to market in one day. Others from further afield lodged at specific inns adjacent to the Market Place. Inns like *The Chough* were the carriers' depots where horses were stabled and messages left. The First World War accelerated motor technology and the village carrier ultimately could not compete with the early buses, but the history of the carrier, often neglected, spanned nearly 150 years and contributed an essential feeder and taxi service.

CARRIERS CARTS
SALISBURY MARKE

152 Hudson described the carriers' carts 'drawn up in rows on rows' in the Market Place 'from a hundred little villages on the Bourne, the Avon, the Nadder, the Ebble and from all over the Plain, each bringing its little contingent'.

IX

An Eventful Century

IN SALISBURY the Great War was greeted by many with enthusiasm; 70 men responded to the initial call up and on enlisting were each given a sovereign. Emotional blackmail was used on local people to persuade their men to go to the Front. If children came home from school crying that 'Daddy is a coward because he did not go to the war then Mother would feel that her husband had failed his country in its hour of need'. Advertisers in the *Journal* went straight on to a war footing. Women were told to shun German underwear, and to show their patriotism by buying British. By the end of 1914, 'useful' Christmas presents being advertised included knife, fork and spoon sets in a canvas case at 2s. 6d. and even barbed-wire cutters. As the war continued there were grim reminders of its reality with increasing adverts for wreaths, crosses and memorial tablets; nearly 3,000 soldiers were nursed at the Infirmary.

Emergency volunteers and a fire service were set up and a branch of Queen Mary's Needlework

153   Recruiting Office, Minster Street. Kitchener's call for men drew a 'splendid response' from citizens who, in a mood of idealism, genuinely believed that the war would be over by Christmas. Seventy men answered the initial call-up request.

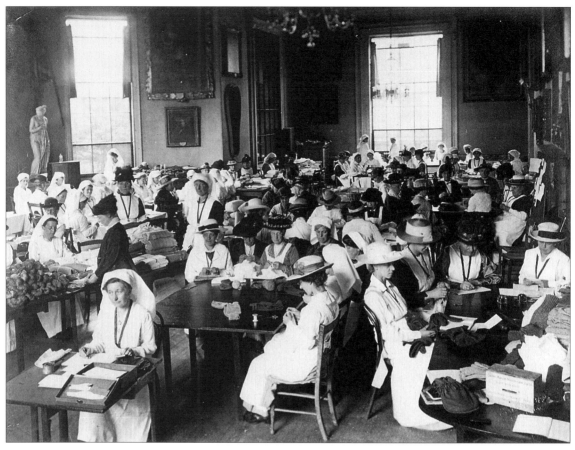

154   *Ladies' Sewing Party. The Queen Mary's Needlework Guild sent a continuous supply of garments and equipment to hospitals, and 'parcels to our fighters'.*

Guild was started in August 1914. The lists of casualties grew as news from the Western Front filtered through, but the press became a channel for propaganda and censorship meaning that Salisbury people rarely understood the horrors of trench warfare. Troops from Salisbury Plain flooded into the city itself and, for off-duty soldiers, town life offered a welcome relief. Trade increased by up to 20 per cent and the Market Place hosted huge military lorries as well as carriers' carts. The streets were 'brown with khaki' and the influx of soldiers seems to have led to an upsurge in 'disorderly houses'. A special women's patrol was established to protect the virtue of Salisbury's womenfolk, while the Women's Emergency Corps dealt with females of

'bad character who are infesting the various military camps'. The success or otherwise of either organisation is unknown!

The *Journal* provides evidence of trials of conscientious objectors but far more emphasis was placed on tales of heroism. Salisbury had its own particular hero in Lt. Tom Adlam. A former pupil of St Martin's and Bishop Wordsworth's Schools, he won the Victoria Cross for his bravery under fire during the later stages of the Battle of the Somme in 1916, in which terrible fighting many Salisbury men died. Despite his wounds, he led a successful assault on a section of the German trench.

Wiltshire was in the forefront of the Women's Land Army. Initially, girls were trained as 'milkers'

155 Wilton's advertisement in the Salisbury Journal. *There was considerable concern during the First World War over the supply of food.*

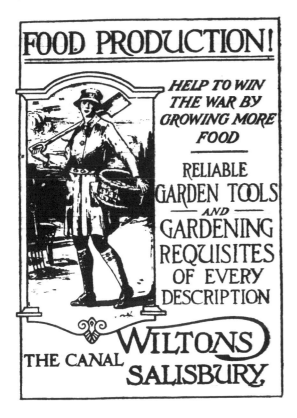

FOOD PRODUCTION!

HELP TO WIN THE WAR BY GROWING MORE FOOD

RELIABLE GARDEN TOOLS *AND* GARDENING REQUISITES OF EVERY DESCRIPTION

WILTONS SALISBURY

THE CANAL

and a dairy school was established at Longford Castle. Later, they enlisted for the duration of the war and received training in different branches of agriculture. Five schools were set up, including one at Wilton House. Edith Olivier described the inevitable problems of recruits who knew little about discipline or farming: 'two of our would be milkers were terrified at the first sight of a cow'. They failed to wear their overalls, patronised the public houses, and did 'the least possible work'. Others, less publicised, settled to farm work and enjoyed the new opportunities granted to women.

The latter stages of the war coincided with a catastrophic worldwide 'flu epidemic, the Infirmary admitting 54 people in one day in November 1918.

Nevertheless, there were huge demonstrations to celebrate the end of the fighting, with an immediate relaxation of lighting restrictions and extra sugar available for Christmas. The Armistice of 11 November 1918 was announced by the mayor in front of the Guildhall. He felt he could say little more than 'thank God the war is over'. A total of 459 men from the city had died and four years later Tom Adlam VC unveiled Salisbury's War Memorial in the Guildhall Square.

Post-war problems facing the city council included unemployment and, especially, a shortage of housing as the war had brought housebuilding to a halt. Lloyd George's commitment to build 'homes fit for heroes' accelerated a building programme in Salisbury and estates of both private and, for the first time, council houses were developed. The earliest council houses were built in Macklin Road, south of the Devizes Road, with those in Wain-a-Long Road and Wessex Road being developed shortly afterwards. Other estates followed and 754 council houses had been built by 1939.

The only general strike in British history took place from 4-12 May 1926. About one thousand railway workers from the Southern and Great

156 Council houses in Wessex Road, built in 1922 and recently renovated.

Western Railways responded to the call to strike but,
overall, the effects on Salisbury were marginal. Postal
services were restricted and Salisbury races had to
be cancelled. A total of 564 men volunteered for extra
duties but only 60 were actually needed including
20 in connection with the railways and six steam
lorry drivers. The British Legion Club opened a
temporary canteen in the Market Place which
provided sleeping and washing facilities for volunteer
drivers and was staffed by women working in four
hour shifts. There were no complaints against the
strikers, food supplies were hardly affected and above

all, there was little evidence of the bitter propaganda battle waged in some parts of the country.

Just as railways had revolutionised 19th-century transport, so motor transport had a similar effect in the 20th century and the consequences for a small medieval city have been considerable and rarely

beneficial. In the early years of the new century 'cyclomania' among the upper classes was fading and motoring was the new craze. Doctors were among the first motorists in Salisbury, and the department store Style and Gerrish ran a 1903 Wolseley. Yet by 1904 only 22 cars and 40 motor cycles were owned by Salisbury residents and it was felt sufficiently significant to be worth reporting that doctors arrived at the scene of the 1906 railway accident by car. W. Rowland, who in 1898 had a cycle works in Castle Street, was hiring out cars by 1906.

Salisbury played a part in the early development of the motor car with its own company, Scout Motors, founded by two clockmaker brothers, Albert and William Burden, in 1902. They outgrew their original site in the Friary and moved to a new factory at Churchfields on the Bemerton Road, producing, in 1909, six models costing between £265 and £730. The peak of Scout output was 1912, with 150 men employed and two 'silent, speedy, superior vehicles' capable of average speeds of 40-50 m.p.h. being produced each week. From 1912 Scout buses were replacing horse-drawn services. Bus firms often began their operations as carriers, such as the highly successful Silver Star Motor Services which ran until 1963. In 1915, Wilts & Dorset Motor Services was founded in Amesbury. Six of their first seven vehicles were from Scout Motors, of a design particularly suitable for narrow country roads. The buses created a minor social revolution and the best companies proved their viability not only with short trips to Salisbury market but over longer distances too. Their heyday was from the 1930s to the 1950s but as car ownership increased so bus services declined.

Car production at Scout Motors was halted during the First World War when the firm was contracted by the government to make munitions. Manufacture was resumed in 1920 but the firm was wound up in 1921 when it became obvious that it could not compete with companies such as Ford and Morris.

160   St Mark's roundabout. The newly built roundabout on the inner-relief road in 1966 looking very free of vehicles. Traffic lights now control the major entry points.

161   Park and ride at the Beehive, Old Sarum, shortly after opening, June 2001. In 1998 another public enquiry approved a park and ride scheme for which construction began in 2000.

The increase in traffic inevitably put pressure on Salisbury's streets. Dusty, muddy roads were first sprayed with tarmac in 1908, a process so successful that the city bought its own machine in 1912. By the 1920s and '30s congestion in the city was becoming acute and the 1930s saw the first car parks (on the site of the present coach station and Salt Lane), parking restrictions, one-way streets, traffic lights, pedestrian crossings and speed limits.

Accidents in the 1930s were common; in 1934 there were 216, with five fatalities. The Chief Constable's Annual Report of 1935 asserted that 80 per cent of road accidents were avoidable, and he recommended heavier fines and imprisonment for motoring offences. Cyclists came in for heavy criticism: they rode three abreast, with no lights, and were often a menace on the road. The bus driver who was fined for dangerous driving in Fisherton Street in 1930 at a speed estimated at 30-40 m.p.h. would be unlikely to achieve even this today. Various solutions to the growing problem of congestion have been planned, debated, altered and suspended

throughout the later decades of the 20th century, and will no doubt continue to be so. Early measures were implemented without controversy, but local groups campaigned for and against more radical proposals. The first phase of the inner relief road was opened in 1966 and did indeed bring some relief to the medieval streets, but the volume of traffic continued to grow. Plans for alternative routes for a true by-pass were published, and reached a public enquiry in 1993, which heard evidence for over a

162   Boots the chemist and Bingham's department store. Window shopping in the High Street in the 1930s.

163   Entertainments provided a diversion from the difficulties of the economy in the 1930s.

year. An eventful outcome in favour of the project was overturned only months later, after the 1997 General Election. Something clearly had to be done. An integrated approach was discussed under a transport study which considered public transport, cycleways, pedestrianisation, as well as alternative traffic management schemes. The 21st century has begun with piecemeal improvements rather than wholesale new ideas.

Unemployment increased during the early years of the 1930s as Salisbury was not immune from the depression felt throughout the whole country. Men queued outside the Labour Exchange in Catherine Street and the mayor organised a local Distress Relief

164   In the summer of 1940, school-based activities were continued through the holidays to keep children together in case invasion necessitated further evacuation. At South Wilts Girls' School, the programme included first aid, gardening, games and music. Here is a folk-dancing session. Note the sand-bag barriers between the classrooms and the quadrangle.

SALISBURY, SOUTH WILTS
AND
BLACKMORE MUSEUM.

Director: FRANK STEVENS, Esq., O.B.E., F.S.A.

School Classes for Evacuated and other
Children.
September 12th——October 31st, 1939.

165   Enrichment of lessons in wartime came from a variety of sources, some proving precursors of modern educational practice. Frank Stevens was well known for the welcome he gave to children at the Museum.

Fund which distributed vouchers for meat, groceries and coal, and parcels of clothing and boots. At Christmas 1933, a tea party was held for the wives and children of unemployed men in Salisbury, but by then the numbers had begun to fall. Seasonal temporary work alleviated the worst for some, and gradually new employment opportunities arose in the area. The Nestlé plant recommenced manufacture of condensed milk and tinned sterilised cream in 1934. The products of multi-national corporations like Coca-Cola first arrived in Salisbury at this time. Tourism depended on prosperity elsewhere but there were sufficient people working in growth industries to maintain a buoyant demand here. The expanding military presence on the Plain towards the end of the decade was regarded with foreboding but did provide increased custom for city shops and services.

As the possibility of another world war loomed plans were made, including zoning the country according to vulnerability to air attack. Salisbury was designated a reception area, contrary to the opinion of the council. The Town Clerk wrote to the government pointing out that the proximity of HQ Southern Command, large military camps and airfields on Salisbury Plain, and of Southampton all made the city a likely target. It was also argued that the high water-table would make impossible the excavation of adequate trench accommodation for the population in the event of air raids. This was all to no avail and at the beginning of September 1939 nearly 2,500 schoolchildren and teachers arrived from Portsmouth as part of the official evacuation scheme. Not all stayed for long, and more arrived later, putting pressure on billeting arrangements, air raid protection, education and other services.

In the schools, shortages of materials, conscription of male teachers, shared buildings and air-raid warnings all disrupted the timetable. In September 1940, Devizes Road School log book recorded that, 'No school could take place during the last fortnight as the buildings were occupied by the military', and, in the following month, the 'timetable could not be adhered to, the staff being engaged in pasting anti-splinter net on screens and lower windows'. At Tower House, where operating facilities were set up for the Emergency Medical Services Hospital in huts on the south-west outskirts of the city, a rota was organised by local doctors to attend whenever the air-raid sirens sounded, but the scheme was abandoned when no casualties arrived. Despite the 'Baedeker' raids on other historic cities, Salisbury was only subject to bomb attack briefly, on two days in August 1942, and even then no one was seriously hurt, though there was damage to property on the western side of the city and in the Castle Road area.

Entertainment was considered important for public morale in wartime, so much so that the job of Chief Projectionist was a reserved occupation. On the afternoon of 11 August, *One of Our Aircraft is Missing* was showing at the New Picture House when the bombs outside supplied real-life sound and vibration effects! The audience was reassured by the staff that all was well and the film continued. In contrast, the flames of burning Southampton were visible to fire-watchers on the roofs of the city. When the Supermarine aircraft factory had to be moved

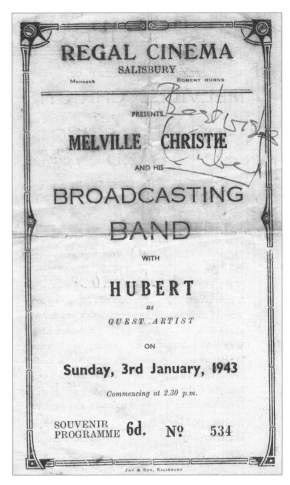

166 *'The proceeds of this entertainment will be handed to the Russian Ambassador for the provision of comforts for the heroic defenders of Stalingrad.' This was one of the more unusual fund raising events in Salisbury during the Second World War. The battle of Stalingrad was reaching its climax in January 1943. The Soviet victory over the German 6th Army was arguably the decisive battle of the war.*

out of danger, some parts of Spitfire production came to Salisbury.

American, Australian and Canadian troops arrived in the area, with chocolate, chewing gum and nylon stockings, and the American Red Cross arranged Christmas parties for all local children. Wilton House, Longford Castle and Breamore House were all taken over by the military authorities. It was impossible for people not to be aware of the build-up to D-Day; heavy convoys disturbed their

167 *Dancing in the Market Place, VE day. Salisbury was good at celebrating national events, and the end of the Second World War was no exception. Church bells rang and there were crowds in the streets under lights which had been dimmed for so long.*

168 *'Prefabs' in Stratford Road were built quickly after the Second World War to ease the housing shortage.*

169 *The peace of Salisbury Close was rapidly restored in 1945.*

night's sleep and camouflaged vehicles were seen in local woodland.

The establishment of the National Health Service in 1948 linked Salisbury Infirmary with the hospital at Odstock which had been built as an American military hospital during the Second World War and was subsequently reopened by Wiltshire County Council. This hugely increased the patient load, staffing establishment, and opportunities for the re-organised hospital service in the area. New departments were created, including orthopaedics, and intensive care. The regional plastic surgery service was based here from 1948 with a specialist burns unit from 1952. This has a world-wide reputation and has trained surgeons from many countries, and the specialist nursing staff have initiated developments such as pressure garments to reduce scarring. Some 20,000 people came to Salisbury between 1946 and 1989 as guinea pigs in the programme of research into acute respiratory infections at the Common Cold Research Unit. Their period of isolation contributed to achievements in the understanding and treatment of these diseases. The limitations of a city centre site and a building with its origins in the 18th century outweighed the advantages of convenient access, and resulted in the move from the Infirmary to a new hospital at Odstock in 1993.

The market and shops in Salisbury have continued to attract customers from a wide area. Branches of Liptons, Co-op, Boots, Timothy Whites and Marks and Spencer arrived, followed more recently by chains such as BHS and Laura Ashley.

170(left) *Thomas Sharp's
futuristic 1949 plan for the city,
as described in his book* Newer
Sarum. *Note the proposed main
road directly through St Thomas's
Square. He also had the progressive idea of converting the old
Town Mill, then an electricity
station, into a museum.*

*171   Floods in St Edmund's Church Street, 1967. Extreme
weather conditions are not confined to recent years. There were
damaging high winds in 1930 as well as 1987, and particularly
heavy snow storms in 1881, 1908 and 1962. In November 1934,
fog was so dense that scouts equipped with torches assisted lost
pedestrians. Salisbury streets were always prone to flooding, notably
in 1883 and 1915, and in 2000.*

The transatlantic notion of a mall first appeared in Salisbury in 1969 with the redevelopment of the chequer behind *The Old George Hotel*, and others have followed. The arrival of out-of-town shopping is witnessed by the traffic queues on the Southampton Road, and in the city centre today there is an interesting contrast of small specialist shops which arrive and depart in a very short time and others which demonstrate a remarkable persistence. While the market is a continuing presence, the individual stalls too show some variation, though many are long-established, each with a devoted clientele. The

172 (left)   Tribbeck's jewellers and watchmakers shop in Bridge Street decorated for the coronation in 1911. This long-lived retail establishment in Salisbury, founded in 1905, is still run by the same family.

173 (below)   Another long-established shop is Watsons, here seen celebrating the coronation of Queen Elizabeth II. The firm has been selling china and glass in Salisbury since 1834. (See also illustration no. 25.)

174 *Art in many forms has always been an important part of the Salisbury Festival. In 1999, 'Two men on a bench' by Giles Penny graced the lawns outside Mompesson House in the Close, drawing a striking contrast between their modern simplicity and the delicate beauty of the 18th-century plasterwork and glassware inside.*

175 *The University of the Third Age is thriving amongst Salisbury's ageing population. Their choice of a sundial to mark the new millennium is appropriate since it both measures and records the passage of time.*

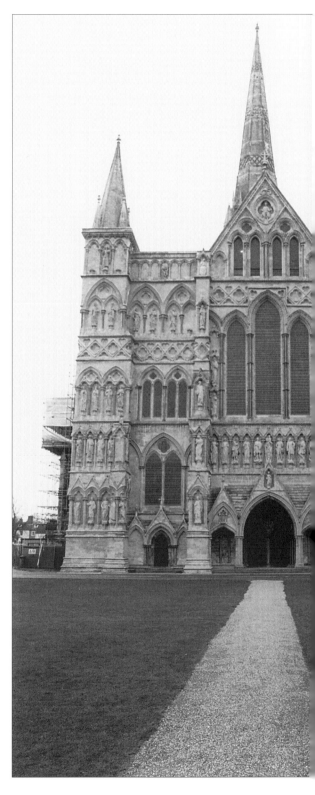

176 *West Front of cathedral after restoration. The appeal to save Salisbury Cathedral's spire from possible collapse was launched in 1985. By 1992, £6.5 million had been raised, and the following year the scaffolding was removed revealing a pristine and even more elegant spire. This project was followed by an ambitious five-year programme to recreate the façade of the West Front.*

ice-cream van, the WI stall, and John Longley's game stall remain perennial favourites. Recent innovations have included an annual visit from French market traders, and a monthly farmers' market.

The 21st century has begun with a flush of new coffee shops and with continental-style outdoor tables around the Market Place. Those with comfortable seats and daily newspapers are providing meeting places and a focus for conversation reminiscent of the coffee houses of the 18th century. Modern Salisbury welcomes visitors from around the world at all seasons of the year, making a significant contribution to the local economy. A notable occasion in the calendar is the Salisbury Festival. The modern festival dates from 1973 but has changed

177 *The last shop in the Friary, 1969. Mrs. Jesse's family had run this general stores from the 1880s until it was demolished to make way for new housing.*

beyond recognition since then. Over the years, it has attracted international artists from the worlds of popular and classical music, put on exhibitions, and above all developed street theatre, fringe events, and magnificent spectacles in the Cathedral Close and Market Place. The Festival of May 2000 celebrated in dramatic fashion the completion of a major cathedral rebuilding and conservation programme with Carl Orff's *Carmina Burana* performed against the backdrop of the newly restored West Front, strikingly illuminated by lights and fireworks.

Salisbury was fortunate in escaping most of the unwelcome attention from developers in the 1960s. The New Street alterations and the infamous, if temporary, elevated 'road to nowhere' over Culver and Gigant Streets were blatant, though rare, examples of bad planning. Unlike other cities, the heart of Salisbury has not been ruined. In the new millennium, much of Bishop Poore's far-sighted vision has survived and Salisbury citizens and tourists alike can enjoy that legacy. The cathedral and town co-exist, the religious and the secular each dependent on the other, as was the case in the 13th century. There is a unity and order about Salisbury. The basis of the city's streets continues to be the medieval

178   Housing in Gigant Street. Several of the old courts have been converted and small, attractive town houses been built, bringing a living population back into the centre of Salisbury.

179   The Michaelmas Fair. A Salisbury fair was first established in 1221 and the October Michaelmas fair has prospered since 1270. This photograph of the late 1920s captures the atmosphere of the steam-powered fair.

chequers. Their frontages have been maintained while the slum areas of the courts have been successfully transformed into shopping malls or housing. Old buildings, like the Infirmary and the brewery, have been reutilised, and the city has retained its attractive mix of architecture. The market and Michaelmas fair

still prosper. There is a sense of permanence; it is a place people find hard to leave, sufficiently near to London for commuters, but with its own relaxed atmosphere.

The decision taken at Old Sarum 'to descend into the Plain' has proved an enduring one. The 13th-century planning concept has meant that Bishop Poore 'would still be able to find his way from the Market to the Cathedral without feeling he had landed on the moon'.

180   *The cathedral from Long Bridge about 1900. The view across the water meadows from Harnham remains much the same as when Constable painted it.*

Select Bibliography

Barrett, P., *Barchester: English Cathedral Life in the 19th Century* (1993)

Benson, R. and Hatcher, H., *Old and New Sarum, or Salisbury* (1843)

Burnett, D., *Salisbury: The History of an English Cathedral City* (1978)

Chandler, J., *Endless Street: a history of Salisbury and its people* (1983)

Chandler, J., *Salisbury: History and Guide* (1992)

Dodsworth, W., *Salisbury Cathedral* (1814)

Dorling, E.E., *A History of Salisbury* (1911)

Hall, P., *Picturesque Memorials of Salisbury* (1834)

Haskins, C., *The ancient trade guilds and companies of Salisbury* (1912)

Hatcher Review

Heape, R.G., *Salisbury: some architecture in the city and the Close* (1943)

Hudson, W.H., *A Shepherd's Life* (1910)

McCarraher, J., *The Story of the City Hall 1937-61* (1998)

Northy, T.J., *The Popular History of Old and New Sarum* (1897)

Olivier, E., *Without Knowing Mr Walkley* (1936)

Ramsey, G.D., *The Wiltshire Woollen Industry in the 16th and 17th Centuries* (1965)

Robertson, D., *Sarum Close* (1938)

Royal Commission on Historical Monuments, *Ancient and historical monuments in the city of Salisbury,* vol.1 [the city] (1980); vol. 2 [houses of the Close] (1993)

Salisbury 200: the bi-centenary of Salisbury Infirmary 1766-1966 (1967)

Salisbury and South Wilts Museum, *monographs*

Salisbury Journal, *The history of a city: Salisbury's first thousand years* (2000)

Salisbury Local History Group, *Caring* (2000)

Sharp, T., *Newer Sarum: a plan for Salisbury* (1949)

Shortt, H. (ed.), *City of Salisbury* (1957)

Slack, P.A. (ed.), *Poverty in early-Stuart Salisbury* (1975)

South Wilts Industrial Archaeology Society, *monographs*

Spring, R., *Salisbury Cathedral* (1987)

Swayne, H. J. F., *Churchwardens' accounts of S Edmund and S Thomas Sarum 1443-1702* (1896)

Victoria History of the Counties of England, *Wiltshire,* vol.3 (1956), vol.4 (1959), vol.5 (1957), vol. 6 (1962)

Wiltshire Archaeological and Natural History Magazine

Index

Numbers in **bold** indicate page references to illustrations

Adlam, Tom, 112, 113
Agincourt, 10, 17, 26
almshouses, 14-16, 53, 77. *See also* individual almshouses
Amesbury, 47, 115
Andover, 46, 47, 68, 70, **81**
Anti-Corn Law League, 84
A'Porte, John, **17**, 23
Arts Centre, 109
Ashley Road, 96
Assembly Rooms, **61**, **62**, 88, 105, 107
Asquith, H.H., 96
asylums, 87; Fisherton (Old Manor), 87-8; Laverstock House, 87-8, **87**
Aubrey, John, 56, 58, 74
Aula le Stage, **35**. *See also* Close
Avon, river, 1, **2**, 4, 8, **18**, **22-3**, 37, 64, 86, 103
Avranches, Henry de, 5,
Ayleswade (Harnham) bridge, **12-13**, 12, 14, 37, 48. *See also* bridges

bakers, 25, 30
Banks, Benjamin, **60**, 60
barber surgeons, **27**, 28
Barbur, John, 25
Barnwell (Barnard's) Cross, 20
Barrington, Bishop, 71
Beauchamp, Bishop, 31, 32, 71
bell-making, 25
bell-tower, 7, 47, **48**, 48, 71, **72**
Bemerton, 74, 88, 95, 105
Bingham, Bishop, 12, **14**, 14
Bishop's Palace, **51**, 52, 55. *See also* Close
Bishop Wordsworth's School, 98, 112. *See also* schools and colleges
Black Death, 21
Blechynden's almshouse, **55**. *See also* almshouses
Blue Boar Row, **18**, 60, 71. *See also* streets
Bodenham, Ann, 52
Bottenham, Agnes, 15
Braybroke, Canon William, **38**, 38
Brewer, Alice, 7
brewing and malting, 25, 44, 45, 74, **75**, 76, 95, 126
bridges, 10, 12. *See also* individual bridges

Bridport, Bishop, 16, 17, 33
Brodie, William Bird, 83
Brown Street, **25**, 41, 45. *See also* streets
Brown Street Baptist church, 99
Bugmore, 10, 44, 64, 86
Butcher Row, 18, **19**. *See also* streets
butchers, 18, 25, 26, 28, 30, **92**
Buterlegh, John, **32**

Campeggio, Bishop, 33
canals and river navigation, 64-5, **66**, 110
carriers, 44, **110**, 110, 112. *See also* roads
Castle Street, 10, **22-3**, **42-3**, 102, 103, 108, **114**, 115. *See also* streets
cathedral, **3**, 8, 12, 25, 30, 33, 37, 46, 52, 64, **110**, 126, 127, **128**; building, 5, 6, 7, **53**, 71, 72, 98-9, **124-5**, 126; choristers, 26, 37, **38**, 58, 90; Dean and Chapter, 28, **31**, 33, 46, 50, 71, 90, 104; music, 37, 58; services, 33, 44, 98, 99; spire, 7, **8**, 52, **124-5**. *See also* bell-tower, Wren, Wyatt
Cathedral School, 37-8, 90. *See also* schools and colleges
Catherine Street, 60, 117. *See also* streets
cemeteries, 86
chantries, 33, 37, 71
Charles I, 46, 50
Charles II, 50, 52, **53**
Charters, 17, 31; 1225, 8; 1227, 9, 10, 18, 30, 95; 1612, 30, 32, 41, 95; 1685, 55
Chartism, 84
Cheesemarket, 19, **22-3**
Chequers, **5**, 8, **9**, 74, 84, 126
Chipper Lane, **100-1**, 101, 107. *See also* streets
cholera, 84, **84-5**, 85
Chough, 110. *See also* hotels, inns, public houses
churches, churchyards, parishes, 99, 103. *See also* individual churches
Churchfields, 6, 115
Church House, 46, **46**, 53, **76-7**, 77-8
cinemas, 24, 107-8, **109**, 119
City government, 17, 26, 41, **95**, 95; corporation, council, 10, 17, 25, 30, 32, 40, **53**, 53, 64, 65, 71, 95, 104, 113; mayor, 17, 30, **32**, 32, **44**, 44, 46, 52, 71, 95, 113, 117; medieval, 25; relations with bishop, 8-10, 17, 25, 30-2,

32, 70; responsibilities and duties, 19th and 20th centuries, 95; Salisbury District Council, 95; 1835 Municipal Corporations Act, 95. *See also* Charters, Tenements

City Hall, 107, 108

Civil War, 46-50, **49**

Clarendon, 7, 25, 47

Close, 7, 13, 25, 30, **31**, 32, **33**, **35**, 35, 37, 38, 44, **48**, 48, 50, **52**, 52, 60, 71, 72, 76, 89, 90, 91, 95, 99, 100, 102, 109, **121**, **124**, 126; wall, 8, **31**, 31, 35. *See also* individual houses, Wyatt

Cobbett, William, 1, 5, 82

College, later Council House at Bourne Hill, **12**, **62**, 95, 103

College of Matrons, **55**. *See also* almshouses, Close

Collins family, 57, **63**

Common Cold Research Unit, 121

Constable, John, **7**, 73, **128**

Council houses, **113**, 113, **114**, **120**

Crane bridge, 12, 65. *See also* bridges

Crane Street, 12, **21**, **46**, 46, 53. *See also* streets

Cromwell, Oliver, 48, 50, 52

Culver Street, 20, 23, 126. *See also* streets

Cutlery, **74**, 74

cycling, 103, 115, 116. *See also* roads

defences, 10, 17; bars, 10; Close wall, 8, **31**, 31, 35; ditches, 10, 26; gates, 10, **10**, 26, **31**, 35, 37, 48, 52, **53**; ramparts, 10, **12**, 12, 13

Defoe, Daniel, **11**, 57

Dereham, Elias de, **7**, 7

De Vaux College, 16-17, **35**, 37. *See also* schools and colleges

Devizes Road, 98, 113. *See also* streets

Devizes Road School, 98. *See also* schools and colleges

Dissolution of Monasteries, 33, **35**, 35, 37

Domesday Book, 2, 4

Education Acts, 98. *See also* schools and colleges

Edward III, 22, **31**

Edward IV, 32

Edward VI, 38

Edward VII, 105, **106-7**

elections, **83**, 83, 96, **97**, 117

electricity, **75**, **88**, 88-9

Elizabeth I, **37**, 40

Elizabeth II, **123**

Ely, Nicholas of, 7

Endless Street, 48, 96, 101, 107, 108. *See also* streets

Exeter Street, **31**, **82**, 100. *See also* streets

fairs, 20, 31, **39**, 95, 98, 126, **126-7**

Farrant, John, 58

Fawcett family, **76**, **83**, 96, 98, **104**, 104

festivals, pageants and celebrations, 30, 33, 37, 104-5, **105**, **106-7**, **113**, **120**, **124**, 125-6

Finch, William and family, **87**, 87-8

fire brigade, 95, 96

First World War, 96, 107, 110, **111**, 111-13, 115

Fish Row, 18, **19**. *See also* streets

Fisherton, 14, 17, 30, **34**, 34, **66**, 74, 78, 83, 88, **92**, 92, **93**, 95

Fisherton bridge, 12, 14, 17. *See also* bridges

Fisherton Street, 12, 64, 74, **79**, 89, 90, 94, 107, 108, **109**, 116. *See also* streets

floods, **122**

friars, 13, **14**, 14, 20, 35, 37

Friary, 6, 14, 99, 115, **125**

gas, 88

General Strike, 113-15, **115**

George III, 72

George Inn, 52, **53**, 123. *See also* hotels, inns, public houses

giant, 28-9, **29**, 30

Gigant Street, 99, **126**, 126. *See also* streets

Godolphin School, 90. *See also* schools and colleges

Greencroft, **22-3**, **39**, 39, 103

Guild of St George, 17, 26

Guildhall, Bishop's, 26, **70**, 70-1; Elizabethan Council House, **40**, 40, **69**, 70-1; Guildhall (present day), 26, **62**, **70**, 70-1, 82, 113; Medieval Council House, 40, 71

guilds, 22, 26, **27**, 28, 30, 37, 38. *See also* separate crafts and trade companies

Halle, John, **23**, 23, **24**, 24, 30, 31, **32**, 32, 73, 108

Hamilton Hall, 90, 107

Hamilton, Bishop, 99

Handel, G.F., 59

Hardy, Thomas, 90

Harnham, 4, 12, **22-3**, 30, 40, 74, 103-4, **128**

Harris, James, **59**, 59, 60, 105

Hatcher, Henry, **32**, 72, 81, **83**, **90**, 90

Hemingsby, **33**. *See also* Close

Henry III, 7, 9, 13

Henry V, 17, 26

Henry VII, 25

Henry VIII, **33**, 33

Herbert, George, 58, 105

Herman, Bishop, 2

Highbury Avenue School, 98. *See also* schools and colleges

High Street, **10**, **61**. *See also* streets

Hobnob, **29**, 29

horse racing, 40, 50, 114

Hospital of St Nicholas, **13**, **14**, 14, **15**, 15, 37. *See also* almshouses

hotels, inns, public houses, 25, 26, 44, 60. *See also* individual names

Hudson, W.H., **22**, **94**, **110**

Hussey, William, **62**, 71

Hyde, Robert, 46

Infirmary, 64, **65**, **79**, **86**, 86, 107, 111, 113, 121, 126

innoculation, 58, 64

Ivie, John, 44-6, **44**, 50, 52-3, 64

James I, 41

James II, 55

Jewel, Bishop, 34-5, 50

Joiners guildhall, **27**, 28

King's House *see* Close, Museum, Training College

Leaden Hall, **7**. *See also* Close
leather, **25**, 25, 26
Leland, John, 4, 10, **12–13**
libraries, 60, **100–1**, 100–2
leisure and entertainment, 58, 60, 77, 102–4, **103**, **108**, **117**, **119**, 119. *See also* cinemas, fairs, festivals, horse racing, libraries, museums, music, sport, theatres, tourism
Lightfoot, William, 23, **28**
Literary and Scientific Institute, 90
London, 38, 39, 44, 57, 59, 60, 68, 70, 84, 86, 91, 92, **93**, 109
Longford Castle, 47, **48**, 48, 58, 60, 65, 113, 119
Lovibond, Joseph, **76**, 76
Ludlow, Edward, **47**, 47, **48**, 48

Macklin Road, 113. *See also* streets
Malmesbury House, **59**. *See also* Close
market, **13**, **18**, 18, 31, 42, 94, 95, 115, 121, 123, 125, 126, 127
market crosses, 19. *See also* individual crosses
Market House, 88, **93**, **94**, 94, 102
Market Place, **18**, 19, **20**, 20, 26, 30, **40**, 41, 47, 52, **69**, 71, 78, 83, 84, **88**, 94, **104**, 104–5, **106–7**, **110**, 110, 112, 114, **120**, 125, 126, **126–7**
Marsh, John, 60
Martyrs, **34**
Mary I, **34**, 34, 37
Maryfield (Myrifield), 6, 7
Maundrel, John, **34**, 34
Mechanics' Institute, 90, 101
Medieval Hall, 109. *See also* Close
Members of Parliament, 5, 17, 30, 46, **59**, 82, 96
Methodism, **99**, 99
Middleton, Andrew, 84, **85**, 86
Milford, **5**, **22–3**, 30, **58**, **73**, 74, 83, 90, 91, 92, 94, 95
Milford Street, 10, 12, 30, 109. *See also* streets
mills, **13**, **22–3**, 89, **122**
Minster Street, 11, **84–5**, **111**. *See also* streets
Mitre House, **10**
Mompesson House, 52, **124**. *See also* Close
Mompesson, Thomas, **52**
Monmouth Rebellion, 55
Montgolfier balloon, **58**, 58
museums, 29, **91**, **102**, 102, **118**
music, 58–60, **60**, 72, 105, 107

Naish, William, **9**, 10, 12
Netherhampton, 20
New Canal, **18**, **23**, **32**, 57, 60, **61**, 108, 109. *See also* streets
New Street, 10, 60, 90, 107, 126. *See also* streets
Nightingale, Florence, **86**, 86
Nonconformism, 98, 109
North Canonry, **8**. *See also* Close

Odstock hospital, 121
Old Castle, 4. *See also* hotels, inns, public houses
Old Sarum, Chap. 1 *passim*, 7, 12, 18, **82**, 82, **103**, 103, **116**, 127; castle, 2, 4; cathedral, 2, 4, 7, **31**; Iron Age, 1, 4; Normans, 1, 2, **31**; Romans, 1, **2**, 4; Saxons, 1, 2, **3**
Olivier, Edith, 113

Osmund, Bishop later Saint, 2, **5**, 7, 25, **26**, 33

Papal Bull, 4, 5, **16**
The Parade coffee house, 60. *See also* hotels, inns, public houses
Parliamentary reform, **82**, 82–8, 96, 98, **104**
Peniston, John, 80
Penruddock, Colonel John, **52**, 52
Pepys, Samuel, 52, 60
Petersfinger, 86
Pheasant Inn, **27**. *See also* hotels, inns, public houses
plagues, 21, 41, 42, **44**, 44
Playhouse, **109**, 109
police, 95, **96**, 96, 101
Poore, Bishop Herbert, 5
Poore, Bishop Richard, 5, 6, 7, 13, 14, 17, 126, 127
Popley, Joan, **41**
population, 21–22, 25, 39, 73, 74, 84, **95**, 99, **126**
Poultry Cross, **ii**, **19**, 19, **27**, 48, **80**
poverty, 39, 41, 42, 44, 52, 77, 81; beggars, 41, **42**; poor relief, 14, 15, 37, 39, 41, **44**, 44, 45, 50, 53, **76–7**, **77**, 78, **78–9**; Poor Law Guardians, 96; Poor Law Unions, 78, **78–9**. *See also* almshouses, John Ivie, workhouses
prisons, gaols, gallows, stocks, etc., 41, **42**, 52, 78, 79, 82
Pugin, Augustus, **24**, 100
Puritans, 41, 30, 44, 45, 46, 50, 53

Queen Mary's Needlework Guild, 111–12, **112**
Queen Street, **18**. *See also* streets

Radnor House, **79**
Radnor family, 58, 64, 71, 83
railways, 70, **73**, 74, 91, 94, 113–4, 115; accidents, **92**, 92, 109–110, **110**, 115; building, 91–2; companies, 91–2; stations, 92, **93**, 110
Rammell, Thomas, 78, 84
Red Lion, 77. *See also* hotels, inns, public houses
roads, 65, 115, **116**; by-pass, ring-road, **116**, 116–7; companies, 115; traffic, 116, 123; vehicles, 110, **114–15**, 115, 116. *See also* carriers, cycling, stage coaches, turnpikes
Roger, Bishop, 2, **3**, 4
Rollestone Street, 103. *See also* streets
Roman Catholicism, 6, 34, 55, **80**, 80, 89, 99, 100
Russel, William, 17

St Ann's Street, 10, **27**, **63**, 102. *See also* streets
Stratford Road, **66–7**. *See also* streets
St Edmund's church, 12, 28, 37, 41, 42, 45, 50, **51**, 109
St Edmund's Church Street, **99**, **122**. *See also* streets
St Edmund's College, 12, 37, 104
St Edmund's School, **89**, 98. *See also* schools and colleges
St Francis' church, 99
St John's Chapel, **13**, 14, 37
St Mark's church, 74, 99, 107
St Martin's church, 4, **5**, 8, 12, 37, 50, **66**, 89, 99
St Martin's Church Street, 100. *See also* streets
St Martin's School, 98, 112. *See also* schools and colleges
St Osmund's church, 100
St Osmund's School, 89. *See also* schools and colleges

St Thomas's church, 12, **13**, 18, **28**, 28, 32, **36**, **37**, 37, 40, 41, 45, 46, 50, 52, 99, **122**, **124**
St Thomas's School, 98. *See also* schools and colleges
Salcot, Bishop, 33-4
Salisbury College, 90. *See also* schools and colleges
Salisbury Exhibition 1852, **75**
Salisbury Journal, 57-8, 65, **68**, 68, **72**, 80, 81, 82, 83, 84, **87**, **110**, 111, 112, **113**, **115**
Salisbury Plain, **22**, 22, **110**, 112, 118
Salisbury Postman, 57
Salt Lane, 99. *See also* streets
Salvation Army, 99-100, **110**
Scammell's Road, 20. *See also* streets
School board, 98
School of Art, 90. *See also* schools and colleges
schools and colleges, 37, 89-90, **90**, 95, 96, 98, 119; medieval schools, 37-8
Scot's Lane, **85**. *See also* streets
Scott, Gilbert, 99
Scout Motors, **97**, **114-15**, 115
Second World War, 95, 118-21, **118**, **119**, **120**
Sherfield, Henry, 45, 50
Shoemakers' guildhall, **27**, 28
Shops and shopping, **17**, 18, 24, 35, **57**, **74**, 111, **113**, **117**, 118, 121, **122-3**, 123, **125**, 125, 126
Silver Street, 19, 26
Southampton, 22, 23, 26, 38, 65, **66**, 70, 91, 118, 119
Southampton Road, 90, 123
South Wilts Girls School, 98, **118**. *See also* schools and colleges
Speed, John, **40**
sport, **102-3**, 103
Spread Eagle, 60. *See also* hotels, inns, public houses
stage coaches, 67-8, **68**, 70, 110. *See also* roads
Stonehenge, 88
Stratford Road, **66-7**
Stratford-sub-Castle, 1, **22-3**
streets, 8, **18**, 18, condition of, 65, 67, 116. *See also* Chequers, individual streets
Stukeley, William, 1
Sunday schools, 89. *See also* schools and colleges
Swayne, William, 10, 23, 24, **28**, 28, 30, 31, 32
swimming pools, 103
Swing Riots, **81**, 81-2

tailors, 26, 28, 30, 37
Taylor, John, 44, 64
Taylor's almshouse, **55**. *See also* almshouses
tenements, 8-9
Teynterer family, 14, **53**
theatres, 60, 107, 108-9, **109**
Theological College, 91. *See also* schools and colleges
Tollgate Road, **73**
Toone's Court, **85**

tourism and visitors, 25, **26**, 40, 118, 125, 126
trade and industry: medieval, 12, 17, 18, 21-2, 23, **24**, 24, 25, 26, 28, 31; 16th and 17th centuries, 38-9, 41, 42, 45, 52; 18th century, 57; 19th and 20th centuries, 73, **74**, 74, **75**, 76-7, 99, 112, 117-18, 119, 125. *See also* guilds, shops and shopping, wool and woollen cloth
trade companies, 30
Training College, **89**, 90, **91**, 96, 102. *See also* schools and colleges
transport and communications, 64-5, 68, 109-10, 114, **115**, 117. *See also* canals, railways, roads
Trinity Hospital, 15, **16**, 37. *See also* almshouses
Trowbridge, 96
Turberville, D'Aubigny, 60, 64
turnpikes, **66**, 67. *See also* roads

Victoria Park, 104, **104-5**, **106-7**
Victoria, Queen, 100, 104, **105**
Vine Inn, 68. *See also* hotels, inns, public houses

Wain-a-Long Road, 113
Wansey, Henry, **76-7**, 77-8
Ward, Bishop Seth, 52, 53, **55**, 60, 65
watercourses, 8, **11**, 21, **26**, 41, **42-3**, 67, 71, 84, **84-5**, 86, **102**, 102
Water Lane, 38
weavers, 26, 28, 30
Wesley, John, **99**
Wessex Road, **113**, 113
White Hart, **67**, 89, 92. *See also* hotels, inns, public houses
William I, 2
William III, 55, 56
Wilton, 1, 4, 6, 12, **13**, 14, 18
Wilton House and Pembroke family, 37, 46, 113, 119
Wilton Road, 96
Winchester, **2**, 4, 10, 22, **58**, 68
Winchester Street, 10, 41, 99
Winterslow Hut, **68**, 68. *See also* hotels, inns, public houses
Wise, Michael, 58
witchcraft and sorcery, 35, 52
women, 28, 41, 76-7, 96, 98, **102**, 103, 111, **112**, 112, **113**, 113, **114-15**
wool and woollen cloth, 19, 20, 21-2, **22-3**, 23, 24, 25, 30, **32**, 38-39, 42, **54**, 74
Wordsworth, Bishop John, 88, 95, 98
workhouses, 39, **41**, 41, 45-6, **46**, 53, **76-7**, 77-8, **78-9**, 86. *See also* Church House
Wren, Christopher, 52, **53**, 60
Wren Hall, 37, **38**. *See also* Close
Wyatt, James, **71**, 71-2, 98
Wyndham family, **62**, 81, **83**, 83

Yarnmarket, 19
York, Duke of, 59